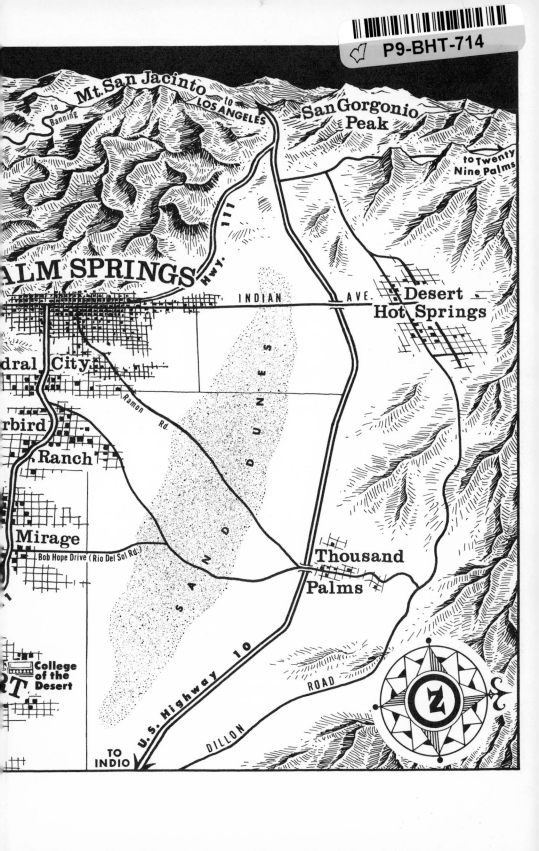

J

DESERT EDITOR

To John Caughey, California's
most perceptive historian,
I offer my aspirant's effort.
With my deepest respect and
admiration.

J Wilson McKenney
9/20/72

Books by Randall Henderson

ON DESERT TRAILS, TODAY AND YESTERDAY
Westernlore Press, 1961

SUN, SAND AND SOLITUDE
Westernlore Press, 1968

DESERT EDITOR

. . . the story of
Randall Henderson
and Palm Desert

by J. Wilson McKenney

Wilmac Press .... 1972 .... Georgetown 95634

Text type set in Caledonia by
Professional Press, Berkeley

Presswork and bindery by
Howell-North Press, Berkeley

PRINTED IN THE UNITED STATES OF AMERICA

CONTENTS

ILLUSTRATIONS:

TO CYRIA

Just Between You and Me

HENDERSON

W H
pu
magaz...
as now conducted, ...
letter appeared, a steady barrage of letters both pro and
con have been coming to the editorial desk.

...on
...ince that

than in a whole semester at school. For Nature is th
greatest artist of all.

. . .

If my old prospector friends Frank Coffey and G
Lederer and Tommy Jones were living today I am afra
they would have to start learning their profession all ov

1. A Man and An Idea

The editor, his work, and his

environment come to focus.

THIS IS A BOOK about a man, an enterprise, and a town. Each element, deserving book-length treatment, molded and catalyzed the other, and it is the purpose of this brief history/ biography to record the resulting interaction covering nearly a quarter of a century. Since our chief concern here is with the interplay of the three parts, it is appropriate that we first introduce the man, with appropriate interpretation. His interests and his physical environment will follow in logical sequence.

In a small Iowa town named Clarinda a boy-child was born on April 12, 1888. There must have been an unseasonable snow fall that day because the infant grew to manhood hating cold country (or astrologers would suggest that he was born under the sign of Aries, by nature fiery, hot, and dry). Nelson Rankin Henderson, Scotch-Presbyterian town druggist, and his wife, Mary Catherine, a Quaker, were the parents of five children, four boys and one girl. The first was named Randall. They grew, as did most middle-class youngsters of the central states, with their faces turned westward. Randall, the oldest, was the first to move west, although all five eventually came together as adults to assume independent roles in creating a community in a cove of virgin desert in southern California.

Randall was an average student in grammar school and high school at Shenandoah, Iowa. He took a healthy interest in sports, learned to play the mandolin, and enjoyed hiking and riding horseback. After school hours he worked for the Henry Field Seed Company, laboring in the vegetable gardens in summer and clerking in the mail order house in winter. He finished high school in 1905, but kept his job for a time in order to save money for a college education.

In April, 1907, not yet 19 years old, Randall appropriated the cheapest transportation then available to get to California— in a well-used but empty cattle car. Through the slatted sides of his moving cell he peered out at the railroad settlements of the West, and he liked his first views of the vast desert lands rimmed by distant purple mountains. He arrived in San Francisco on the first anniversary of the great earthquake and fire. Through the summer he held a job with the Buckingham & Hecht Shoe Company, and in September he traveled to Los Angeles to enter the University of Southern California.

With various jobs he worked his way through U S C, waiting table, washing dishes, painting houses. He held the school welterweight wrestling championship for two years, captained the varsity basketball squad, and served as student body president in his senior year.

He reminisced later that perhaps the most significant act of his student life was to take a part-time job as a sports reporter for the Los Angeles *Times*. The ace reporter and columnist, Harry Carr, had an adjoining desk, and he advised Randall to become a country newspaperman. In 1911, with a bachelor's degree packed in the bottom of his trunk, he headed for Parker, a village on the Arizona bank of the Colorado River. After a brief interval as a surveyor's helper, he took a job at 25 cents an hour as a printer's apprentice at the weekly Parker *Post*. He wrote news, solicited advertising, learned to operate the Linograph type-setting machine, and helped with presswork. Within the year he returned to Los Angeles to marry Vera Riopel, the daughter of the painting contractor who had employed him during his college years. They set up housekeeping in a small house in Parker.

The *Post* contained news of Palo Verde Valley, and copies of the paper were dispatched weekly by horseback to be delivered in Blythe. His employer sent Randall to Blythe to handle the news and advertising sales. Within months the young apprentice had found a partner, Myron Watson, and they set up their own print shop to publish the Blythe *Herald*. The small enterprise grew. My mother became the office bookkeeper when Randall left town in 1918 to complete his pilot training for service in World War I. On his return to Blythe after the Armistice, Henderson resumed the editorship, but in 1922 he and Watson bought the daily Calexico *Chronicle*.

As narrator, it is necessary for me to introduce myself at this point. I was a barefooted schoolboy, not yet old enough to join the Boy Scouts, when uniformed Lieutenant Henderson returned to the *Herald*. My chief interest was exploring the sandhills and levees near my desert town, an interest which shifted to examining the movements of the impressive young officer/editor. When I completed my schooling twelve years later— marked by an almost exclusive interest in the school publications— I became Henderson's front office apprentice at the *Chronicle*. In 1933 we became business partners when I went to Calipatria, Imperial County, to edit and publish the weekly *Herald*. Our partnership continued when we founded the *Desert* Magazine in El Centro in 1937, a relationship which terminated two years later.

The writing of this book was not my original idea. Randall had spent the last year of his life on it, until his heart gave out on July 4, 1970. He was 81 years old when he began work on a manuscript which he proposed to title "Palm Desert, Yesterday, Today, and Tomorrow." He left a file of responses to questionnaires, notes, clippings, letters, and other memoranda. He had written two chapters and portions of others, indicating that he was interested in recording history, not autobiography.

His widow, determined to carry out Randall's intent that the book be completed and published, asked me to assist. His daughter, Evonne Riddell, and her mother, Vera, supported Cyria's request that I undertake the job. I studied the files and talked with responsible residents of the Coachella Valley community.

At first, a logical approach suggested that I edit the drafts on hand and add pertinent material that could be readily verified. But the limitations of writing contemporary history by a non-resident author seemed to me to be insurmountable. Only 26 years had passed since stakes had been pounded into the sand for construction of the *Desert* Magazine plant, the first modern building south of the highway. The community which sprang out of the sand near the publishing headquarters was still too young to justify the perspective of a meaningful history. Observing the rapid pace of events in the community, I was sure that anything I could put in print would be obsolete before the ink dried, although I tried to bring material on significant public institutions and movements up to date.

Previous commitments prevented me from starting work on the book for six months, although correspondence and research continued for nine months. I needed the freedom to write what I knew best, a story largely *about* Randall and his evolving philosophy. By assuming authorship our dilemma seemed to be solved, but I had also compounded my responsibility. I discovered that it is a debilitating experience to write *about a friend.* The temptation was strong to describe my subject as a giant in his time, and a counter impulse to ignore the credit due him. Honesty required me to write about the whole man I knew, neither saint nor sinner, but a man whose stalwart character was nurtured by the land in which he labored.

Although I have written for publication all my adult life, my credentials for producing a book-length work are limited. But Randall and I had shared our lives for nine years and our correspondence had covered four decades. Out of this living experience I should have opportunity to interpret with greater validity than would be possible for a researcher of the future having only access to old documents. I can hope that readers will not discover that my talents have not matched the opportunity.

Correspondence between Randall and me after my departure from *Desert* Magazine, especially before and during the Palm Desert move, was detailed and extensive; the three-inch file is a documentary revealing Randall's hopes and purposes. He was twenty years older than I (lacking five days), and we came to have very nearly a father-son relationship. Regularly through the decade of the 30s— and periodically thereafter— we climbed, hiked, and camped together in desert places, and some of the ideas we discussed around campfires are reflected in parts of this book.

Parts of this work, especially those portions concerning acquisition and development of the first Palm Desert land and his exploration of neighboring palm canyons, are recorded here in substantially Randall's words; I simply converted them to third-person viewpoint. It has been my conscious effort to write in Randall's style— with obvious limitations— and I have inserted personal observations only when necessary to illustrate a point.

Randall Henderson was introverted, self-contained, self-reliant, and not always an easy man to know. In speech, he was often inarticulate when he tried to reveal the humanitarian principles which in his late years dominated his thoughts, but when he talked informally at campfires his language could be colorful and precise. In business matters he was usually hard-headed and rigidly conventional, always the slave of his promise and the conscience of his debt. In matters concerning his social responsibility he was self-effacing and studiously receptive of ideas; his reading in sociology and economics was prodigious. In his relationships with people he was often uncompromising and severe, or he could be courteous and friendly, but never gregarious. Considering himself a "hunt-'n-punch reporter," he could rise to eloquence on a subject of his choice when alone with his typewriter. Normally undemonstrative, the lines of his face could reflect self-contained joy or anger.

Scornful of intemperance, he never touched alcohol, ate simply, and detested the cigarette habit which claimed him most of his life. Awed by the wonders of the natural world, from the tiny sprouting seed to the majestic panorama of mountains, he had no tolerance for the looters and despoilers. He loved the open spaces and solitude; he could tolerate the teeming cities only with dogged determination.

Most of Randall's literary effort— other than the perceptive editorials he wrote for his newspapers— is locked in

12,000 printed pages of *Desert* Magazine. He didn't remake the society of men, but he informed, inspired, and encouraged thousands of readers who gave him their loyalty and respect. He had always worked hard, and he slowed down only a little between the time of his retirement and his death twelve years later. He wrote and published two excellent books on his desert observations and experiences, wrote an unpublished book on the socio-economic problems of our national life, and expended his energies in support of his ecological principles.

Randall was the father of a boy and a girl. Evonne, circulation manager of *Desert* 1942 to 1946 and 1953 to 1958, has been manager of the College of the Desert bookstore since the opening of the institution. She is the mother of two children: Randy, graduate of USC, and Jeanne, graduate of San Diego State College. Randall Jr. (Rand) was killed in battle at Saipan in 1944. Randall had long hoped that his son would succeed him in the magazine business, and the young corporal's death brought the father "'a great loneliness." It is evident that Randall, at the age of 56, returned from his military service in Africa to plunge himself into Herculean labors in order to compensate partially for his loss.

This opening chapter, properly an introduction to "Mr. Desert" and an explanation of how and why his book came into being, would not be complete without appropriate acknowledgement of support and assistance.

Randall had clearly indicated that he intended to dedicate the book to Cyria, and it is, quite properly. His wife, talented sculptress who worked professionally in the British Empire before her marriage to Randall on March 18, 1949, is the real inspiration for this book. Without her energy and interest it would never have been written and published. She and I regret that it is now impossible to acknowledge the aid of innumerable people who assisted Randall during his inquiries on local history; it would be unfair to print only the names we found in his preliminary notes. We regret, too, that much of the material generously offered could not appear in print.

We have sought advice, notably from Ole Nordland, friend of Randall's since the 1940s, former editor of the Indio *News*, now secretary of the Coachella Valley County Water District, and chairman of the Riverside County Historical Commission. Jack Pepper, present editor of *Desert* Magazine, and Hal Kapp, president of the Palm Desert Library Board, have also been helpful. But if errors of judgment or fact appear in these pages, we cannot hold our advisors accountable.

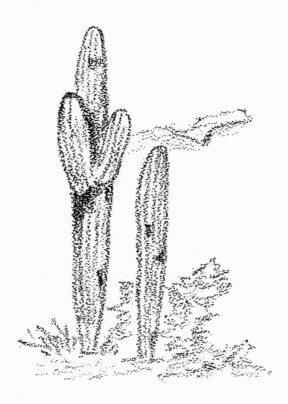

RANDALL HENDERSON

"Mr. Desert"

1888 - 1970

Randall Henderson (left), Malcolm Huey, and the author (right) begin a three-day climb up the east face of Picacho Diablo in the San Pedro Martir range of Baja California, March 21, 1935.

Randall Henderson (right) with the author on the peak of Santa Rosa Mountain. A pre-cocked camera shutter snapped this picture at noon on June 8, 1936. This was the day the two men decided to launch *Desert* Magazine.

Aerial view of *Desert* Magazine building at Palm Desert, taken as construction was being completed in the spring of 1948. Highway 111 in the foreground is now a divided eight-line super-highway; curving El Paseo is a principal drive through Palm Desert. Unoccupied areas are now covered by commercial establishments, homes, and landscaped gardens.

2. This Was Cahuilla Land

Before white men came, Indians
developed a hardy culture
in Coachella Valley.

SIXTY-ONE YEARS AGO young Henderson— with an A.B.
degree buried in the bottom of his trunk— arrived in the
desert country. His first job after arrival in Parker, Arizona,
was with the U.S. Land Office, surveying boundaries and
staking out ten-acre allotments for each of the Indians on the
Colorado Indian Reservation. The allotment idea proved to
be a bureaucratic mistake from the standpoint of both the
Indians and the Bureau of Indian Affairs, and it was eventually abandoned.

But during the months he walked the mesquite-covered lands of the reservation he became deeply interested in the life of the Indians, and he came to know some of them personally. During the later years of his editorial work— particularly in coverage of Chemehuevi, Cocopah, Havasupai, Navajo, and Hopi for *Desert* Magazine,— this interest continued through correspondence and visitation.

He became fascinated by the experience of desert tribesmen in finding and preparing food, especially among those isolated groups that depended entirely on plant and animal life indigenous to arid lands. He liked to report his observations, especially when talking to young people at campfire councils, of the harvesting and preparation of mescal. He had visited a group of Pai-Pai Indians at the Arroyo Agua Caliente in Baja California, where he had eaten cooked mescal for the first time.

The mescal plant, he would explain, is botanically classified as *agave deserti*, and it provides both food and fuel for the Indians. Agave grows in upper and lower Sonoran botanical zones, and it flowers only once in its lifetime, thus receiving the common name of century plant.

His visit to the Pai-Pai was in May, and many of the agave plants growing in the area were nearing the end of their life spans. They had grown large buds somewhat resembling enlarged heads of asparagus. The Indians used long sharpened sticks to gouge the buds out of roseates of needle-pointed blades. When extracted, the edible part of the mescal bud was shaped somewhat like a pineapple.

Preparing for the roast, the Indians dug a pit about thirty inches deep and three feet wide which they lined with rocks. They ignited a wood fire in the pit which burned until the rocks were well heated. They placed a mescal bud or buds among the hot coals, added more rocks, and covered the pit with sand. This process was completed in late afternoon, and the next morning the pit was opened, the buds removed, and the charred husks stripped off. Each bud was well cooked, it had the color and consistency of cooked yams, and had about the same flavor.

In response to questions, Randall drew heavily on his reading of the anthropological literature on Indian lore, particularly concerning the life and habits of the Cahuilla tribe which inhabits the Coachella Valley. He was also able to report on his observation of charred rocks of ancient mescal pits in and near Palm Desert, leading him to believe that roast mescal was a staple diet for prehistoric tribesmen wherever the plant grows. Part of the material in the remainder of this chapter is extracted from notes and quotations in his files.

Margaret Boynton was author of a book published in the 1930s, *Stories and Legends of the Palm Springs Indians*. She recorded a story recounted to her by the Cahuilla chief, Francisco Patencio. The aged chief said that many of his people came over the pass from the west, led by five tribal headmen:

"The head man was tired and sick and lame. He took his staff of power and struck it into the ground. He twisted it around and caused the water of a spring to come out. Then he went into the water and cured himself, and his people also. Then the people separated again to different places. Some went up into the Santa Rosa Mountains, some went to Palm Canyon, and others went to Seven Palms. Most of the people stopped at Indian Wells."

This was tribal legend, handed down from generation to generation. We know that the original name of Palm Springs was Agua Caliente, and the hot springs still bubble out of the ground there, though captured by white men. Even if we could accept the old chief's miracle story, no clues remain regarding the migration he described. The original naming of the springs would suggest Spanish influence, which would have been after Father Junipero Serra's entry into Alta California after 1769. The name "Agua Caliente", incidentally, still applies to the Indian reservation set aside by the federal government in 1896 (26,523 acres, including much of the present city of Palm Springs).

Separation of early migrants into groups which moved into adjacent areas is significant, movements probably caused by relative scarcity of food and water. The visible water supply at that time was the small and erratic streams which flow down the eastern slopes of the San Jacinto and Santa Rosa Mountains and the floods which thunder down the same stream beds during infrequent storms.

Scattering of his people, as stated by Chief Patencio, is confirmed by modern ethnologists who identify the Cahuilla by habitat: Pass, Desert, and Mountain. The area (western San Gorgonio Pass to Salton Sea or Sink) is bounded on the north by the Serrano and Chemehuevi, on the west and south by the Luiseño and Diegeño, and on the southeast by the Kamia and Yuma. Differences in these groups, basically of Shoshonean origin, were largely linguistic, but there were differences relating to character and intelligence which gave the Cahuilla marked advantages in the battle for survival.

Harry C. James, resident of Lolomi Lodge, in the area of the stronghold of the Mountain Cahuilla in the San Jacinto Mountains, is author of five books on Indians of the southwest, including *The Cahuilla Indians*, published by Westernlore press in 1960. An intimate of the Cahuilla, he offers some significant clues:

"The best index to Cahuilla intelligence and imagination is their folk-lore, highly poetic and broadly cosmic. Any thoughtful examination of their artifacts also proves that intelligent and imaginative minds guided their hands, and further, that they are by no means afraid of hard work. To shape the solid granite manos and pestles and mortars with the symmetry and finish which many of their utensils show requires craftsmanship of a high order— and unstinting labor. To make pottery as graceful as many of their ollas, and baskets as beautiful in design as theirs are, demonstrates intelligence, artistry, and industry."

Dr. David Prescott Barrows, for many years president of the University of California at Berkeley, in his doctoral thesis, *The Ethno-Botany of the Cahuilla Indians of Southern California,* suggested other factors which may have caused these people to migrate into this seemingly barren and sterile land. Barrows came to the area as a 19-year-old student in 1891. In subsequent years, as a guest in the homes of these Indians and as a student of the environment in which they lived, he became intimately acquainted with their economic and social life.

"The absence of food in this desert land," he wrote, "is more apparent than real.... I cannot pretend to have exhausted my study of the food supply of these Indians, but I have discovered not less than sixty distinct products for nutrition, and at least twenty-eight more utilized for narcotics, stimulants, or medicines, all derived from desert or semi-desert localities."

One of the most abundant sources of food for the prehistoric dwellers of this desert land was the mesquite tree. The fruit of the honey and screwbean mesquite is a legume, pods from three to six inches long. Cahuilla women gathered the pods in great quantities during summer months, spread them in the sun for thorough drying, and stored them in elevated basket granaries. The beans were not shelled, but pods and seeds were pounded into meal with mortar and pestle. The meal, rich in sugar and protein, was soaked in water and served in many ways, both raw and cooked.

Among other plants which yielded food were chia—a species of sage—pepper grass, and some species of cactus.

The fruit of the pricky pear members of the cactus family was especially favored. The lower slopes of the mountains which rim the Coachella Valley yielded many nutritious foods in season. These included sumac, agave, manzanita, and wild plum or apricot.

At higher elevations the Indians gathered pinyon nuts, acorns, elderberries, and the fruit of the juniper. Acorns and pinyon nuts were staple items, and the desert tribesmen made annual pilgrimages to mountain areas where oak and pinyon grow. Many of the well-preserved trails which lead from the floor of the Palm Desert cove to levels above 4000 feet were made originally by desert Cahuilla on harvesting expeditions to the area now known as Pinyon Flats.

Where water was available the Cahuilla cultivated small patches of corn, beans, squash, and melons. Corn Springs, ten miles southeast of Desert Center in the Chuckawalla Mountains, was probably once a source of water for the cultivation of Indian gardens. When white men first visited the Corn Springs oasis in the early 1900s a generous supply of water flowed from the spring. Gus Lederer and Tommy Jones, jackass prospectors who lived there many years, used the spring to irrigate their gardens. The spring is surrounded by a stately group of *Washingtonia* palms, and adjacent boulders are adorned with the petroglyphs of prehistoric tribesmen who once grew some of their food there.

While the squaws gathered and processed native vegetable foods for the use of their families, it was the male responsibility to hunt for meat. James wrote: "Community rabbit hunts were held frequently. Cahuilla men and boys, armed with bows and arrows and throwing sticks, would circle out through the desert, and they would usually return with dozens of cottontails and jackrabbits."

Deer and bighorn sheep of the higher regions were also fair game for hunters until the competition of white hunters armed with guns made big-game hunting fruitless. Four of the larger animals, the grizzly bear and jaguar (both of which are now extinct in southern California) and the mountain lion and coyote, were regarded by the Cahuilla as sacred relatives.

William Duncan Strong, in his *Aboriginal Society in Southern California,* tells the story of a small party of men who came upon a female grizzly and two cubs near where Beaumont is today. The old Indian man in the party spoke to the bear quietly, explaining to her that they meant no harm, so she should not bother them. Without further ado the three animals went away peacefully.

Barrows reported that three refreshing beverages were generally in use among the Cahuilla when he was residing with them. The most popular of these drinks were made by mixing the crushed seeds of mesquite with water. Other drinks were made from the leaves of sumac and from the petals of the ocotillo blossom. Ephedra (Mormon tea) grows widely in this area, and it was believed to have medicinal value. All beverages reported were non-alcoholic. A tea made from creosote (*Larrea mexicana*) was believed to be a remedy for tuberculosis, and for coughs and pains of the chest.

Two members of the Mountain Cahuilla, Ramona Lubo and Juan Diego, became Ramona and Alessandro in the famous book by Helen Hunt Jackson. *Ramona,* written in 1884, now recreated annually by the people of Hemet and San Jacinto in a pageant-play, brought to national attention the serfdom and brutality to which Indians of southern California were subjected by the mission system and white settlers. Incidents of the novel were drawn from actual events witnessed or investigated by Mrs. Jackson. The graves of Ramona Lubo and her husband are marked in an old Cahuilla cemetary near Anza.

The names of two great leaders of the Cahuilla remain

fixed in tribal lore and in the histories written by white men. The name Cabezon (meaning "large-headed" in Spanish) was given the wise leader of the Pass Cahuilla during early Spanish rule in California. Old Cabezon befriended owners of large land grants in the western valley and he assisted them in many ways. He is said to have been the Indian chief who assisted William D. Bradshaw in locating the San Bernardino-La Paz wagon road which served the 1862-70 gold rush to the Ehrenberg area on the Colorado River. The third descendant of the Cabezon dynasty is said to have died at Chino canyon near Palm Springs in the early 1900s. The name survives (now spelled Cabazon) in a railroad station, a post office, and a mountain, all in the eastern slope of the San Gorgonio Pass.

Juan Antonio was the best-known of the great Cahuilla chiefs, probably because he served brilliantly as a war leader for the Californios during the Mexican period. Don José del Carmen Lugo, who held a Mexican grant of 29,000 acres where San Bernardino now stands, retained Juan Antonio as a kind of chief of police assigned to guard Cajon Pass against raiders who came down out of Mojave Desert. Lugo had suffered heavy losses of horse herds to marauding Utes, and Antonio proved to be an effective guardian.

The great valley lying west of San Gorgonio Pass was generally regarded as Serrano territory, but Juan Antonio and his band of fifty to eighty warriors lived there for many years and they were granted land for their services. Early records describe Juan Antonio as a man of great dignity, short, heavily muscled, and wiry, with the look of an African lion about his eyes and forehead. General Kearney once addressed him as General, and thereafter he wore a military emblem on his coat. A white settler in San Timoteo Canyon testified that "he was accorded more absolute respect and deference by his people than we show to the President of the

United States. The word of such chiefs as Juan Antonio and Manuelo of the Luiseños was law. They were natural leaders, and kept absolute order among their people."

When the Mormons completed the settlement of the San Bernardino area, they paid the Cahuilla for their rancheros, and the Indians moved eastward to San Timoteo Canyon and Yucaipa Valley. With the increasing intrusion of white settlers onto these favored lands, the Indians slowly moved into the mountains and desert.

The Pass (or Western) Cahuilla had a precarious existence, living in comparative isolation. They took jobs as servants to the whites, and their exposure to smallpox and other white man's diseases caused rapid reduction of population. By 1920 the remnants of the Pass Cahuilla were living at the Morongo Indian Reservation east of Banning.

In 1970 the Riverside field office of the Bureau of Indian Affairs reported that there were 1,044 Indians residing on tribal lands, five reservations set aside by the federal government for the Cahuilla. The report lists names of the reservations, date of authorization, and acreage:

Agua Caliente (Palm Springs), 1896, 26,523 acres.
Torres-Martinez (Toro), 1876, 31,695 acres.
Augustine (Thermal), 1891, 615 acres.
Morongo (Banning), 1876, 76 acres.
Anza (Santa Rosa Mountains), 1875, 18,272 acres.

The Bureau refers to all of these Indian groups as "Mission Indians," although the influence of the Spanish mission padres was negligible; the "savers of souls" visited the desert infrequently. Archeologists have not uncovered evidence of permanent religious structures in this area.

Dates for the creation of reservations are coincident with increasing interest and activity of white men in Coachella Valley. The U.S. Congress demanded shortly after California became a state that a survey be made for a southern railroad route. The Williamson-Blake survey of 1853 demonstrated that the San Gorgonio Pass was the best low-level passage on the entire Pacific slope, and the segment from San Bernardino to Yuma was favored by the Southern Pacific Company, although construction did not begin until the late 1870s.

In this period white settlers in the pass demanded soldier protection from the "depredations" of red men, and a treaty was signed with the Indians, but it was never ratified by the Congress. The Indians became wards of the state, and land was set aside for them. The S.P. rails reached Indio in 1876, the year that the Torres-Martinez reservation north of Salton Sea came under the jurisdiction of the Department of the Interior. The railroad company, pushing its lines to Yuma the next year, employed large numbers of Cahuilla men to grade roadbeds and lay rails, and to harvest mesquite wood for engine fuel. The Indians proved to be industrious and they were physically well-adapted to hard labor in the desert climate.

The first white men to buy land in the Palm Springs area arrived in 1880. "Judge" John Guthrie McCallum became a settler in 1884, purchasing a one-fifth interest in the original townsite of Palm Springs of 320 acres on March 24, 1885. More settlers came in the early 1890s, including "Dr." Welwood Murray of Banning, who built a small wood and adobe hotel near the hot springs. Mild desert winters and the therapeutic values of the hot springs brought visitors, and by 1913 there was a small general store, a post office, and a number of tent houses. Much of the land was in government reservation, and the Cahuilla refused to sell to the newcomers. However, they rented or leased acreage as demand grew for resort space, thus beginning real estate operations which proved to be lucrative for the tribe. As white men exerted pressures for investment in desert lands the tribe employed legal counsel, and there were bitter and prolonged court battles. James wrote, "to watch the alert, well-groomed Agua Caliente Tribal Council is to realize that here are Indians who will not be trading Palm Canyon for a string of shell beads."

A few years ago Congressman John V. Tunney (now Senator) of Riverside prompted an investigation of Indian claims and counter claims. Testimony revealed that as much as 44 per cent of Indian income from extensive desert resort holdings had been spent in fees to court-appointed conservators and legal guardians. As a result the Bureau of Indian Affairs was directed to assume a more alert guardianship of federal trust lands, and to take over control of impounded assets. During the last half-century the Cahuilla has learned to be on guard against encroachment. The tribe, now reduced to a very small population, is believed to be among the most prosperous in the United States.

The first aborigines to come to the desert country sought life-giving water (the first priority of all desert dwellers in succeeding decades). They lived on the shores of ancient Lake Cahuilla or Blake's Sea (whose beach line once reached north and west of the present site of Indio) and the lake not only provided palatable water but an abundance of clams and fish. But when the in-flow of the Colorado River was diverted toward the gulf by the natural silting at the river's mouth, the lake (now Salton Sea) began to dry up and became increasingly saline.

John W. Hilton, the desert artist, lived for many years at Thermal, and he publicized his theory that the Indians had procured palatable water by digging in the beach sands, and later by digging at grassy seepages along the base of the hills. Hilton wrote in 1936, "These were undoubtedly the first wells in the Colorado Desert and were probably dug somewhere near the old site of the Toro village. Some of the older diggings still visible may be the remains of those ancient wells. They are found south to Fig Tree John's and north as far as the present Indian Wells near Point Happy, where a populous Indian village once thrived." Nordland reports that "near the Fish Traps a venerable mesquite tree has grown over the center of an Indian dug well, probably the only present evidence of this type of well. It is hidden and camouflaged from the casual visitor."

A well from which the city of Indian Wells drew its name had a trench more than fifty feet long which descended to a depth of about twenty-five feet. A pool of water formed at that depth. Squaws walked down the slope to carry out water in ollas or water-tight baskets which they balanced on their heads. There is no evidence that water from these wells was used for irrigation.

In the years after gold discovery at La Paz in 1862 feeding and watering stations of the Bradshaw Road were established at Indian Wells and Toro; the route would not have been feasible without these water sources. With continued usage after 1870 the county of Riverside dug a windlass-operated well near the old Indian Wells site, which continued in use until about 1910.

Modern newspaper writers have speculated that several thousand Indians lived at Indian Wells at one time, but scientists believe that no more than 200 to 300 could have survived in the area— and this would have been one of the largest concentrations of the Cahuilla. Shards and stains of ancient fires in canyons of the cove communities suggest that many Indians lived nomadically, presumably during seasons of water availability.

Basketry and pottery are prized by modern museums as examples of the relative artistry and craftsmanship of the Cahuilla, believed to be some of the best of the California tribes. Barrows recounts his personal observation of basket-making: "The old woman holds her unfinished basket in her lap; at her right lies a pile of grass for the body of the coil and on her left side, soaking in a little pot to keep them pliable, are various colored withes. Her only instrument is an awl made of bone or from a long spine of opuntia cactus set in a piece of asphaltum for handle. No model or pattern is ever used; the basket takes shape under her skillful fingers, and is always symmetrical and shapely, and the intricate regularity of the pattern carefully preserved. The patterns are varied and always graceful."

George Wharton James, in his book *The Wonders of the Colorado Desert* (1906), described the pottery-making process he observed: "They find the clay in the mountains, soak it and then puddle it with round rocks. As soon as it is properly worked, the pottery-maker takes a piece of the clay, rolls it out into a long rope, and then begins her coil just as if she were making a round basket. One coil is laid upon another and the two are pinched together, then smoothed out with a small bone, wood, or gourd-shell paddle. When the vessel is complete it is dried in the sun for a short time and then put in a fire of mesquite wood. Firing is a difficult process and requires watching closely. Sand is thrown upon the fire when it seems to burn too rapidly."

The language used by Dr. Barrows in describing the early Cahuilla is generally reflected by other writers on this subject: "I am certain that from any point of view the Cahuilla Indians are splendid types of men and women. Physically, they are handsome, often large of size, many men six feet and over, with splendid shaggy heads, and faces of much command and dignity.

"Their desert home has given them great powers of endurance and enormous toleration of heat and thirst. With rare exceptions—and those only among the young men who frequent the settlements—they are absolutely honest and trustworthy. Their homes and their persons are orderly and clean. The fine pools and springs of warm mineral water which are common throughout their habitat are prized possessions.

"Their splendid wells, unique among the Indian tribes of America, their laborious irrigation of maize, their splendid community life with well-built homes and basket granaries, their effective pottery, their exquisite basketry, their complete and successful exploitation of all the plant resources throughout hundreds of square miles of mountain and desert, these achievements are significant evidence of a people of high cultural integrity."

3. Then Came the Explorers

The Valley was unappreciated
until the dawn of America's
westward movement.

A VAST DESERT wasteland— that was the impression most Americans had of southwestern United States during the first half of the nineteenth century. There is no record of American "discovery" of the arid lands north of Salton Sink prior to 1850.

However, for three centuries the governors of Spain and Mexico had sought sporadically to extend Spanish influence in the western world by conquest and exploration. In futile searches for "La Gran Quivira," fabled cities of gold and precious stones, the King of Spain sent navigators and horsemen northward from Mexico City during much of the sixteenth century. Hernando Cortez, conqueror of Mexico, was determined to track down ancient stories of Califa and her Amazonian subjects on "the island of California." Captains of the tiny vessels that explored the California coast and the Gulf of California were Mendoza and Beceria (1532), Ulloa (1539), Cabrillo (1542), Cermenho (1596), and Viscaíno (1602).

Most significant in the history of the inland desert were the discoveries of Hernando de Alarcón, who sailed the Gulf of California in 1540 and embarked small boats 200 miles or more up the Colorado River, and Melchor Diaz, who sent out exploring parties from the mouth of the Colorado to bring back the first eye-witness reports of a vast desert wasteland.

Father Eusebio Kino trudged hundreds of miles from inland Mexico to the mouth of the Colorado; his writings confirmed evidence that California was firmly attached to the mainland of the continent and that Lower California was a peninsula, not an island. An intrepid explorer on foot was Father Francisco Garcés, who reached the Yuma Indian villages in 1768. Probably on advice of his Indian hosts, Garcés walked northward along the bank of the Colorado before turning westward across the Mojave desert, the same route he used eight years later when he discovered the great valley of the San Joaquin.

Juan Bautista de Anza crossed what is now Imperial Valley in 1774 and 1775 to colonize San Francisco, but he pioneered a route through Borrego Valley and Coyote Canyon, miles south of Coachella Valley.

Father Junipero Serra founded the mission at San Diego in 1769, then laboriously extended the chain northward to

Sonoma. The Spanish period of California history effectively ended with the Treaty of Guadalupe Hidalgo in 1848. About 1820 padres of the San Gabriel mission established a rancho in San Gorgonio Pass, but the influence of the Franciscans in the desert was brief and there is no recorded evidence that they explored the Coachella Valley.

Historians have recorded the stories of old ones who described the annual spring-time "jornado para sal," beginning as early as 1815, in which oxen-drawn carretas moved from the Los Angeles pueblo through San Gorgonio Pass to the Salton Sink in order to bring back salt for the mission chain. A few years later the record indicates that Cocomaricopa Indians were employed to carry mail between San Bernardino and Tucson, using the Pass route.

The diary of Brevet Captain José Romero has been recently discovered, containing graphic descriptions of the land and Indians he observed in desert journeys of 1823 and 1824. His party moved through the Pass to Agua Caliente, then by way of Toro and Fig Tree John's they reached Yuma. Apparently directed by the viceroy to find a viable transportation link between Sonora and the Mexican settlements in California, Romero returned to report that the desert route was "completely impracticable."

John Charles Frémont, "the Pathfinder," made four overland trips to California in the middle 1840s, but he chose the Mojave crossing or passes in the Sierra. Jedediah Smith, Ben Williams, and other trappers turned their solitary steps as far west as the Colorado, but they told no tales about the desert area we know as Coachella Valley.

In the record of nearly eighty years since the beginnings of civilization along the California coast the arid lands from Mt. San Jacinto to the Colorado River remained a blank on the maps. The few literate observers who had seen it had nothing good to report. Their reasons were simple, and widely advertised: there was no water available at appropriate travel intervals. It wasn't until about the time California achieved statehood in 1850 that reports began to appear about the bountiful hot springs at Agua Caliente, but this was not enough to encourage travelers to attempt the hazardous trip from Yuma to San Bernardino.

The deprecatory comments of two early explorers will illustrate the general attitude toward the desert southwest. At the time of the Gadsden Purchase of 1853 Kit Carson was quoted as saying that the land was so barren "a wolf could not make a living on it." The same area now contains a great city, a dozen smaller towns, rich mining and cattle properties, and five national monuments.

Five years later Lt. Joseph C. Ives was sent out by the War Department to explore and report on the Colorado River and its contiguous territory. In his report he wrote: "The region last explored (the Grand Canyon of the Colorado) is of course valueless. It can be approached only from the south, and after entering it there is nothing to do but return. Ours was the first and doubtless will be the last party to visit this profitless locality. It seems intended by nature that the Colorado River along the greater part of its lonely and majestic way, shall be forever unvisited and undisturbed." Today the people of seven states fight over the water and power resources of the Colorado River, many prosperous towns line its banks, and more than a million visitors a year sign the guest registers of the National Park Service at Grand Canyon.

The opinions of Carson and Ives were echoed in hundreds of ways in the diaries of the argonauts who joined the gold rush to California's Sierra; they persisted in less degree until the beginnings of twentieth-century technology.

Dr. Oliver M. Wozencraft, an Indian agent, came to the desert later known as Imperial Valley in 1849 to dream of the agricultural empire he might create by irrigating with Col-

orado River water. Other strong men of vision followed him—
Rockwood, Perry, Heber, Chaffey— and their dreams and
their fortunes were nearly shattered by the rampaging river
in 1905-6 when it refilled the ancient lakebed we know as
Salton Sea. None of the pioneers lived to see the creation of
the All-American Canal and the Coachella Valley extension
which brought life-blood to the "date garden paradise."

Unseen and unrecorded were the jornados of simple
Sonorans, often travelling on foot, who in 1849-54 were lured
by stories of gold in the Sierra. The record remains only in
unmarked graves along the western edge of the Chocolate
Mountains.

When California was admitted to the Union in 1850,
the first legislature created twenty-seven counties, and San
Diego County covered all the southernmost part of the state.
It wasn't until 1893 that Riverside County was carved out,
containing Coachella Valley and extending from the Santa
Ana River to the Colorado River. Nobody really cared much
about the hundreds of square miles at the eastern end of the
new county because only transient prospectors lived in the
area. As late as the first World War desert land— even
near Palm Springs— sold for two dollars an acre, and the
buyer often felt he had been cheated.

The first genuinely exploratory entries into Coachella
Valley were dictated by the need for transcontinental rail
routes. Lt. R. S. Williamson was directed by the War Department to survey a feasible route for a southern rail line in 1853.
He found that the 2300-foot elevation of San Gorgonio Pass
afforded fewer engineering obstacles than did the mountain
passes to the north. Later, 1872-77, the Southern Pacific built
its transcontinental line from San Gorgonio to Yuma on the
route surveyed by Williamson and party. Completion of the
rail facility marked the beginnings of Indio and other valley
communities.

The scientific member of the Williamson party was William Phipps Blake, 27, a graduate of Yale. He studied the geology, mineralogy, and archeology of the desert lands, then sparsely inhabited by Cahuilla Indians. He named the valley—and areas east and south—the Colorado Desert, taking his clue from the red silted soil. He studied the salted pool at 250 feet below sea level, as well as the ancient beach line which skirts the valley and extends southward into Mexico. Intrigued by discovery of fossils and great oyster shells along the shoreline, he concluded that the desert basin had in prehistoric time been a prolongation of the Gulf of California, or that the river had filled the basin periodically until the silt deposit at its mouth formed a natural dike, thus stopping the back-flow. The dike had grown more than forty feet above sea level, thus accounting for the present position of the ancient beachline above sea level. Certain of his scientific evidence, Blake named the ancient sea Lake Cahuilla, thus honoring the people who had once lived and fished along its shores. His conclusions have never been challenged.

Another transportation feat was accomplished because of the discovery of gold at La Paz on the Colorado in the spring of 1862. Seventy miles north of Yuma on the Arizona bank and 206 miles east of San Bernardino, La Paz could be reached only by an unmapped route across an inhospitable desert. The first news of the find reached the California pueblos in time to take precedence over disturbing rumors of a war between the states. William D. "Bill" Bradshaw, a seasoned miner and veteran of Frémont's California Battalion, set out to explore and mark a feasible route for a staging and freighting line to the river. Bradshaw said he had the advice of old Chief Cabezon of the Cahuilla, who drew a map on the sand, showing how to pass around the Oricopa Mountains and find water holes on the way to the river.

Passing over San Gorgonio Pass with a stop at Whitewater, Bradshaw moved along the eastern edge of the mountains to Agua Caliente, then on to Indian Wells. At Toro, near the northern edge of Salton Sink, he found similar dug wells. The spring at Dos Palmas was an important stop, then up long, sandy Salton Creek wash to Canyon Springs. Water could be found in season at Tabeseca Tanks, then there was a longer pull to Chuckawalla Well. It was an even longer dry run from there to the river until later operators of the stage line dug to potable water at Chuckawalla, Mule Springs, and Wiley's.

A significant value of the Bradshaw Road was that it introduced hundreds of travelers to Coachella Valley, and stimulated a great deal of newspaper publicity about the area. The staging road continued in operation for fifteen years, until the Southern Pacific began operation of trains to Indio.

Although the Williamson survey report of 1853 was not published until four years later (with Prof. Blake's detailed description of the Valley), proponents of a southern rail route urged President Franklin Pierce and the U.S. Senate to clarify the disputed U.S.-Mexican boundary line in order to establish a right-of-way. James Gadsden, minister to Mexico, negotiated with President Santa Anna, and a treaty was finally proclaimed in June, 1854. They agreed to an international boundary running approximately west from El Paso to Nogales, thence northwest to the Colorado River south of Yuma. Mexico ceded about 30,000 square miles (more than one quarter the size of the present state of Arizona) for $10,000,000, or less than two dollars an acre. On this disputed land Americans have built the cities of Tucson, Douglas, and Nogales, as well as many smaller towns. Although the Purchase was completed primarily for the purpose of building a railroad, actual construction of the line was postponed for twenty years due to the need for boundary surveys, unrest prior to and during the

Civil War, and continuing troubles with Apache Indians.

A railroad survey party, having worked its way over San Gorgonio Pass, reached the present site of Indio in March, 1872. In the spring of 1876 construction crews followed; by midsummer trains were able to move from Los Angeles to Indio. By September 1877 the rails had crossed the new bridge at Yuma.

Construction of the rail line and establishment of stations required the drilling of water wells, and this invited the first hardy settlers to Coachella Valley. Non-railroad lands were opened to homesteading, and in 1885 the first farmer had completed his claim.

Exploration of Coachella Valley, as indicated in this chapter, was confined to the relatively brief period between Spanish-Mexican rule in California and the dawn of the industrial age in which Americans were able to dispel the ancient image of "a desert wasteland." The Mexicans ignored the valley; settlers did not follow the few explorers who had seen the land. Overland trails followed routes where a horseman or a span of stage mustangs could find water and grazing at the end of a day's travel, a convenience not found in Coachella Valley, at least not during the early years of the westward movement.

In time team-drawn wagons and buckboards laboring along sandy, rutted roads gave way to high-speed automobiles on wide, paved highways. Powerful grading equipment, submersible pumping systems, and air conditioning, as well as radio, television, and convenient marketing eventually brought to the arid lands all the comforts of metropolitan living. Long before smog became a major health hazard in the coastal cities desert dwellers found a land of far horizons, clean air and unclouded skies, and a mild winter climate.

Our story, then, quickly moves from the lethargy of the Indian and Mexican periods into the dynamism created by

American technology. For it was the resourcefulness and productivity of Americans in this century that made the wastelands habitable; they account for the existence of Palm Desert today.

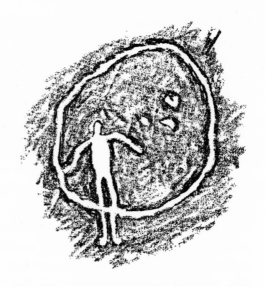

4. Water for A Thirsty Land

*Absence of potable water postponed
early development, but modern man
tapped bountiful sources.*

SURVIVAL of the Cahuilla and the first white settlers in the
Valley, as described in the last two chapters, depended on
availability of good water. With the exception of meager
runoff of streams in the eastern slopes of Mt. San Jacinto and
the Santa Rosa Mountains, there were only four or five watering places used by the Indians in all of Coachella Valley. Agua

Caliente (Palm Springs) was the best known, and there were a few dug wells. Sources at Whitewater on the flanks of San Gorgonio also provided good water table penetration and there was a small seepage at Thousand Palms.

A government survey in the fall of 1875 and the spring of 1876 was conducted by Lts. George Wheeler and Eric Bergland, primarily for the purpose of investigating water sources and feasibility of using Colorado River water for irrigation. They found the water at Agua Caliente sulphur-tainted, alkaline, and 126 degrees of temperature. They were more impressed by the dug wells at Indian Wells and Toro, leading them to believe that relatively shallow drilling would produce useful flows of water. Wheeler's report was in part prophetic:

"The unfortunate climate in which this portion of the Southwest is at present treated by the hand of nature is likely to retard its rapid settlement, even if water was plentifully available; still at some future time in the settlement of the west, each cubic foot of the waters of the Colorado is likely to become valuable in agriculture, mining, and other pursuits..... The soils are of arable nature, needing only moisture to be made productive."

The report was filed in Washington the year that the steel rails of the Southern Pacific reached a place called Indian Wells (later the city of Indio), and fourteen years after Bill Bradshaw had pioneered his wagon road from San Bernardino to La Paz. Indian Wells had been an important stopping place for the hundreds of gold-seekers on their way to the placers before and during the War of Secession. The ancient wells were still useful to the first railroad crews who worked their way through the desert.

Indian Wells, now commemorated by an incorporated city of the same name, was located north of present Highway 111 and east of Miles Avenue junction. The Coachella Valley

Pioneer Society and the Riverside County Historical Commission have marked the approximate location with monuments on Highway 111. The original well dug by the Cahuilla was a large pit at least thirty feet deep with an incline used as a footpath from the ground to the pool of seepage water. Irrigation of gardens was very limited because of the great labor of carrying water in ollas. Early writers reported that the Indians had to repair the well frequently because of damage caused by floodwaters of the Whitewater River.

Similar wells were at Toro northwest of Salton Sink. Both locations were tremendously important to the Cahuilla and to early white travelers.

Operation of steam-powered locomotives required large quantities of water stored in elevated tanks beside the rails. Contractors employed by the railroad company sank wells at various locations along the line, and they hit artesian flows near Mecca. Having a bounteous supply without pumping was an unexpected bonanza, and it caused an increase in applications for entry on public lands. Throughout all the below-sea-level areas of the Valley there were steady artesian flows for several years, but as draw-off increased pumping installations had to be added. Palm Desert, at 238 feet above sea level, never had artesian wells, but adequate supplies were tapped with deep pumping.

Importation of date palm seedlings by the U.S. Department of Agriculture began in 1890, but improved varieties of offshoots were brought in from Algeria, Iraq, and Egypt after 1900, and they adapted quickly to the Coachella Valley climate. With a historical record of only three inches of annual rainfall (and little or no rain from April through September), and an annual average maximum temperature of 88.3 degrees F., conditions for date culture were better than at any of the five other subtropical experimental stations in the United States. Average daily maximum temperatures at

Indio for a twenty-five year period ranged during June, July, August, and September from 100.6 to 106.5 degrees F.,— with very low humidity— providing ideal conditions for maturing and harvesting dates.

The rapid growth of the date industry in Coachella Valley after substantial planting in 1911-22 required tremendous quantities of fresh water. Bearing gardens on lighter soils are usually irrigated every seven to fourteen days during summer and every twenty to thirty days during winter. Experience in the Valley indicates that not less than nine to twelve acre-feet of water per year are necessary for palms in full production, and that twelve to eighteen acre-inches per month are required during summer.

Official 1970 estimates showed 4,152 acres of dates grown in Coachella Valley (and only 200 acres elsewhere in California and 200 acres in Arizona). Citrus and vegetable crops also thrived in the valley, increasing the demand for ground pumpage. Date production reached 45,000,000 pounds a year, representing a major share of the valley's economic stability. Survival of agriculture depended on continued availability of water, and growers became worried by the skyrocketing costs of irrigation as wells sunk deeper and deeper.

Ole J. Nordland, secretary of the Coachella Valley Water District, has prepared for this chapter a hitherto unpublished record of the well-drilling in the Palm Desert area and a study of pumpage for a thirty-year period in the Whitewater River sub-basin.

He counted eighteen wells drilled before 1919 in the area bounded by Bob Hope Drive (formerly Del Sol Road) to Washington Street (Point Happy) and south from Country Club Drive to the mountains. There was considerable drilling from 1917 to 1922, "then a quiet period in the late 30s with another stimulation in the 1940s." The area indicated is roughly the township of T5S, R6E, thirty-six square miles, which includes the present sites of Palm Desert and Indian Wells.

About 1910 Walter Schmid was the owner of a well drilled north of Highway 111 and west of Cook Road, and may be the first of record in this area. Bob Blair was the driller (the record shows that Blair drilled the first half-dozen major wells in the area prior to 1917). Nordland identified well owners prior to 1919, including A. Chapin, E. B. Densmore, C. E. Cook, George Coombs, Charles Thomas, Krutz family, Harold McKenzie, A. F. Grier, W. H. Hayhurst, Conroy Date Garden, George Jenks, Battary Well, W. S. Frey, Art Thomas, E. S. Morrow, Mrs. C. F. Saunders, and Capt. John F. Faulks.

Most of these wells were located north of the present highway, and some were on homesteads which were later abandoned. In 1924 the Palm Desert Community Services District drilled several wells in Section 16 to serve most of the area north of the highway. Dateland Mutual Water Company drilled in Section 21 in 1926 and 1932. Other owners prior to 1940 included Frank Mandel, H. L. Cavanagh, T. W. Braun, and James Arkell.

The record adds the names of twenty well owners in the 1940s, more than half of them owners of land south of the highway. They include the Panorama Mutual Water Co., and Palm Desert Corporation. The Palm Desert Country Club Estates drilled wells in the early 1950s.

A 1971 water resources study made by the Geological Survey of the U.S. Department of the Interior shows that the Palm Desert area pumped 3,240 acre feet of water in 1936, and that this figure nearly doubled (6,080) in 1946. Following World War II, to satisfy the needs of home building and recreational development, pumping increased to 15,600 acre feet in 1956. Nordland stated that pumping in the Palm Desert area was in excess of 24,000 acre feet in 1971. This compares with the 1967 record of 14,400 acre feet at Palm Springs, 5,860 at Thousand Palms, and 6,850 for the Indio area.

It is interesting to note that the first settlements in the upper Coachella Valley were in the coves near the mountains where protection from prevailing winds and availability of good water made habitation desirable. Many wells between Indio and Palm Springs have been pumped for fifty years or more, but many have been deepened because increasing demands have lowered water tables.

The subsurface reservoir from which Palm Desert draws its life-giving water has been receding at an average rate of 1.2 to 2 feet per year, while in the Palm Springs sub-basin the rate has been nearly four feet a year. Water district gauges show present pumping levels range from 125 to 275 feet in the Palm Desert area, and from 275 to 350 feet in the Silver Spur subdivision. Static levels and drawdown from Date Palm Road to Windy Point range from 350 to 550 feet. The pioneer Schmid well drew water at fifty feet in 1911; the twelve-inch casing is now more than 500 feet deep, requiring the use of a ten horsepower motor for pumping. This is the well still in use just north of Highway 111 and about a half-mile west of Cook Road.

Fifty-four years ago, when agricultural demands on available water began to accelerate, valley residents became convinced that development and control of an adequate supply would require a vast cooperative program involving taxation and bonded debt. On January 5, 1918, by a vote of 324 to 49, the people approved creation of the Coachella Valley County Water District; the first board of directors took office in May. The principal function of the new governmental body in the early years was to protect primary water sources of underground tables from private impoundment and to seek augmentation of the supply.

The feasibility of bringing Colorado River water to serve the below-sea-level valleys of the southern California desert was first envisioned by Dr. Oliver A. Wozencraft in 1849. As a regional Indian agent he made a trip to the mouth of the Colorado, and his examination convinced him that the arid region from the Mexican border to the Salton Sink could be made productive with irrigation. He tried to promote his dream through several sessions of the Congress, but his claim for a grant or subsidy was never validated during his lifetime.

A half-century later, when engineering studies confirmed feasibility of the Wozencraft petition, the California Development Company was formed in 1901 to install an intake on the west bank of the Colorado below Yuma and to begin diverting water for irrigation in the valley they named Imperial.

A great ridge of sand, the Algodones dunes, proved to be a serious obstacle to the construction of a canal leading directly from the river to lands to be served. For economic reasons Engineer C. R. Rockwood and his backers decided to detour the big ditch around the southern tip of the dunes area in Baja California. The Mexican government granted the concession, providing that Mexican farmers in the rich delta region would have a right to share in use of the water. There was no impairment of the resulting treaty during nearly fifty years that the original Alamo canal served farmers on both sides of the international line.

The Imperial Irrigation District had served the irrigation and domestic needs of the lands south of Salton Sea for many years by the time Coachella Valley began to put its cooperative plan into operation. Leaders of the water service districts in the adjoining valleys joined their influence and talents to secure a permanent and improved distribution system from the Colorado River which would serve the expanding needs of both valleys. They found sympathetic support in Senator

Hiram Johnson and Congressman Phil D. Swing. Years of political pressure and litigation were necessary, however, involving the water rights of the several states in the Colorado basin, before the Swing-Johnson bill was approved by Congress in December, 1928. The bill authorized construction of Hoover Dam, a diversion dam upstream from Yuma, and an All-American Canal.

The multi-million dollar construction job of the intake and canal was started by the U.S. Reclamation Bureau in 1934, and the 80-mile channel and distribution laterals were completed four years later. Building of the mammoth Hoover Dam was under way at the same time.

A contract for construction of a 123½-mile branch of the All-American canal was signed in 1939, as Hitler's armies marched on Poland. Delays due to wartime shortages of materials and manpower postponed the extension construction along the eastern shore of Salton Sea, and it was not completed until 1948.

The critical importance of the Coachella Valley extension cannot be exaggerated. It had been thirty years since the creation of the cooperative water control system, and during that three decades pumping had pushed deeper and deeper into the earth. A supplemental water supply was badly needed.

Engineering studies and construction of distribution and control systems required several years, a time of anxious waiting for farmers. But the addition of new surface waters for irrigation and the improvement of underground water tables eventually brought new economic incentives to valley growers. The 1967 county agricultural report showed the value of date harvest at more than nine million dollars, with grapefruit adding a value of five and a half million. Various varieties of grapes raised valley income by nearly sixteen million, and the lowly carrot chalked up another five million. With 52,867 acres in production and an estimated crop value of $972 per acre, 1970 agricultural income was set at $51,396,104, the highest for any major irrigated area in the West.

In 1947 voters of Coachella Valley approved a $13.5 million contract with the U.S. Bureau of Reclamation to construct an underground distribution system, a drainage system, and a flood protection system. Two years later the first water from the canal extension entered the underground system near Thermal. An additional loan was approved by voters in 1964 to provide improvement of the canal system in the valley, including reservoirs and water supply systems. The new 136-acre Lake Cahuilla near La Quinta is a major facility of this program, providing not only water storage but public recreation.

As a further safeguard to provide for future supplemental water, the Coachella Valley County Water District entered a contract with the State Water Project for 23,100 acre feet of water to be conveyed from northern California, a gigantic system now being constructed. The Desert Water Agency of Palm Springs has signed for 38,100 acre feet in addition.

Since World War II the phenomenal growth of residential and recreational construction between Indio and Palm Springs— causing the area to be known as "The Golf Capital of the World"— required consolidation and improvement of small water companies that had drawn on underground supplies. The District entered domestic service operations in 1961, beginning by acquiring the Rancho Ramon Water Company near La Quinta. On October 1, 1963, it purchased the Palm Desert Water System.

Ole Nordland, previously mentioned as a contributor to this chapter, was editor of "Golden Years," an 88-page history published by the District in 1968, a source containing valuable historical highlights. In answer to questions regarding future District activities, Nordland commented:

"On acquiring the Palm Desert system, the District replaced major water mains with mortar-lined steel pipes and added reservoirs and wells. The Cahuilla Hills area formed an improvement district in 1966 and began receiving water from the District. The next year the District acquired the Palm Desert Country Club Estates system as well as the Eldorado and Rancho Palmeras systems. In 1969 it bought the Palm Valley Water Company (Harold Hicks property) serving Indian Wells and the country club areas of that community.

"The District has made studies of drainage and flood control systems, has built levees and flood protection dikes. It has maintained the Palm Valley Flood Channel on the west side of Palm Desert to the Dead Indian Canyon area west of Highway 74, and the Deep Canyon Channel on the east side which goes through Eldorado and Indian Wells Country Clubs. It has made reconnaisance studies of sewage and wastewater problems in the area from La Quinta to Cathedral City, and has a master plan for water development in the area.

"New improvement districts have been organized north of the Whitewater River Channel to serve the area from west of the Eisenhower Medical Center and Country Club Drive to Cook Road; sewer and water lines were being laid in 1971. The District's responsibilities have grown over the years in response to the wishes of valley residents. It now serves the area in water conservation, storm water protection, domestic service, sanitary sewer and reclamation systems. It demonstrates a vital and intimate interest in the development of the valley through these vital functions."

Ole concludes with "'this is a land for people with skill and determination." Certainly the record shows that this desert was transformed by men with strength and imagination, men who wanted to raise their families comfortably in a land formerly conceived as a hopelessly forbidding wasteland.

5. "Friend or Stranger, You Are Welcome Here"

The editor moves Desert *Magazine to a barren cove, and that became the beginning of Palm Desert.*

A MILESTONE DATE in the history of a fledgling community of Coachella Valley was July 14, 1947, the official opening date of the new United States Post Office in Palm Desert. A place-name conceived informally two and a half years earlier had become a spot securely fixed on official maps.

Designation of this promising desert subdivision as a new link in the U.S. postal system was in reality a climactic event in a long series of contributing factors. The transformation of this sunny cove at the base of southern California's Santa Rosa Mountains into a potential location of a new American city began in November, 1944, when a publishing team decided to locate its operations in this plot of desert. *Desert* Magazine, then published in El Centro, had outgrown its quarters. The staff needed more space, preferably in an uncrowded desert area which could provide an appropriate backdrop for its editorial themes.

Desert Magazine has played such a decisive role in events which charted the way to the Palm Desert of today that the imagination and resourcefulness of its editor—and subsequent development resulting from his actions—deserve appropriate attention at this point.

Founding of *Desert* Magazine at El Centro in 1937 had been an indirect result of the economic tailspin of 1929-35. Randall Henderson was then publishing the daily Calexico *Chronicle* in Imperial County and I was publishing the weekly Calipatria *Herald* about forty miles north of Calexico. We both had tough going in those depression years, and profits were small or nonexistent. Henderson's problems were more acute because he operated in a town of 5,000 population with a large percentage of Spanish-speaking residents, consumer buying was at a low ebb, and advertisers lost interest in using newspaper advertising space. Randall often had difficulty in meeting his payrolls, even at the low salaries current at that time, and he was usually in debt to his banker. Despite the drastic economic remedies proposed during the New Deal, recovery was very slow.

As business partners, we often talked about our dilemma. We desperately needed a more lucrative potential, and our thinking often turned to starting a magazine, although we were well aware of the mortality rate among special-interest regional publications. How we launched *Desert* Magazine is recounted in the next chapter; this discussion will be more concerned with the business development of the enterprise and its eventual flourishing at Palm Desert.

The first issue of *Desert* came out of the bindery in November, 1937, with only 618 subscribers paid in advance. We printed 7,000 copies. I had spent much time on the road, obtaining potential sales commitments from newsstand distributors, and I shipped several thousand copies on consignment to cities from San Francisco to El Paso. Newsstand sales— at 25 cents a copy— were better than we had anticipated, and introduction to new readers through unit sales helped to account for the increase in subscriber income during the early years.

Finding revenue from sale of advertising space was much less promising. After long and fruitless sales trips through Arizona and southern California, I often returned to the office to report to my partner that I had been able to sign up only enough insertion orders to cover the costs of my travel. I always carried my sleeping bag, shaved at service stations, and ate crackers, cheese, and fruit bought at roadside stores. Selling space in a publication which could not yet show evidence of mass consumer circulation was a discouraging task. Partial compensation for my failure I found in opportunities to do field interviews and get photographs for *Desert* editorial features.

Randall had turned over the operation of the Calexico *Chronicle* to a group of associates in order to buy a commercial printing plant in El Centro, the Elite Printing Co. We had sold the Calipatria *Herald* in the spring of 1937 and I had moved my family to El Centro to begin my duties as business manager of the magazine.

Two years later— on May 12, 1939— Randall and I dissolved our partnership because I found it impossible to continue in the pioneering effort without salary; my savings from the sale of the *Herald* had been exhausted. With my family of four we returned to newspaper business in northern California. Randall was able to assume publication losses with his profitable printing business, later eased by acquisition of my interest by Tazewell Lamb and Bess Stacy. The publication did not show a small profit until August 1941.

Four months later the Japanese attacked Pearl Harbor. Randall had served as an Air Corps pilot in World War I, and he retained a commission in the Air Forces Reserve; he began preparations to return to active duty. A year later he passed his physical examinations and reported for duty at Air Transport Command in Santa Ana, California. Early in 1943 he reached his overseas station at Accra Air Transport Base in the African Gold Coast (later to become the Republic of Ghana). His son, Rand, had earlier enlisted in the Marine Corps, losing his life in battle on Saipan, July 7, 1944.

During Randall's two-year absence from *Desert* Magazine Lucile Harris, now Mrs. Harold Weight, was acting editor. Lucile had been the only employee during my brief tenure, and she had served variously as circulation manager, proof reader, poetry critic, housekeeper, and editorial assistant. The late Bess Stacy carried on as business manager, and Evonne Riddell, Randall's daughter, managed the book store. Marvin Wieben, printshop foreman, had long been a Henderson employee, and he was an effective manager of the back shop. This organization operated the publishing and printing business so competently that Henderson found a large bank balance on his return to civilian life. He was able to move toward reality the dream he had often written about at his post in the African desert: to erect a publishing plant that would meet the requirements of a fast-growing enterprise. A measure of Randall's gratitude is shown in the record that

Lucile, Bess, and Evonne acquired equities in the business on his return from Africa. Marvin became owner of the printing business in El Centro.

At Accra Randall was assigned as Special Services Officer, and his duties included arranging for transportation of enlisted men into "the bush" for recreation and exploration. He studied the life styles of the natives in the Sahara desert and learned much about the topography and flora of the arid lands. His editorial pages for *Desert* Magazine (his "Just Between You and Me" column had appeared regularly in his newspapers and magazine since 1920) reflected his interest in many phases of African desert life. The isolated outpost gave Randall long periods of relative inactivity which he used to plan the future of *Desert* Magazine. His letters during this period indicate that he believed the publishing business should be moved away from city streets into an area that would more directly symbolize the basic philosophy of the magazine.

From his African base on November 23, 1943, Randall wrote me: "I believe I outlined somewhat more specifically in my last letter the notion I have been mulling over of selecting a blank site on one of the most traveled of the southern California desert highways, and there founding our own small desert community, built around the magazine and the printing establishment. My thoughts in this case always turn to that link in the desert highway between Coachella and Banning." Nine months later, August 29, 1944, his thinking about location was becoming more specific: "Naturally I am formulating a lot of plans for *Desert* Magazine after I am a civilian again, including a possible move to Coachella Valley a little later. I rather doubt if Lucile will be able to sell me the Tucson idea now, despite the fact that I have had that in the back of my mind for many years. The advantages of being close to the heart of this great southern California population loom very large in my thinking just now."

The magazine was only four years old—September 8, 1941, when he wrote: "The thought occurs to me sometimes that perhaps *Desert* Magazine should be moved eventually to a more favorable location climatically." And to indicate that our mountaintop "hour of decision" was never far out of his mind in regard to location, he wrote on June 17, 1942 that "sometime in July I shall take my annual pilgrimage to the Santa Rosa Mountains."

Clifford Henderson, Randall's younger brother, was a colonel in the Air Force. He made an inspection tour of the North African wing of the Air Transport Command and visited in Accra for a few hours. Randall told Cliff about his post-war plans for *Desert* Magazine, including his hope that he could find a location where appropriate housing could be provided for the magazine staff. Cliff had been promoter of the National Air Races in the early 1930s and he and his brother Phil had built the Pan Pacific Auditorium in Los Angeles into a profitable enterprise. He commented that he might be interested in a real estate investment in the area that Randall might select, and he asked that he be informed as plans materialized.

Randall's service in Africa included duty in Algiers under General Eisenhower and eight months as officer in charge of a small refueling station at Atar in the Sahara desert. He received his honorable discharge in Washington October 20, 1944. On terminal leave, he was still in uniform when he attended the annual convention of the California Newspaper Publishers Association at the Los Angeles Biltmore Hotel. There he met Ray Gabbert, an old friend who had been publisher of the Riverside *Enterprise* but who was then engaged in the newspaper brokerage business. Henderson told Gabbert about his plans to relocate *Desert* Magazine and mentioned that he was interested in Coachella Valley as a possible location. Ray expressed enthusiasm for the idea and promised to help find appropriate property.

Gabbert knew the owners of property near Cabazon in San Gorgonio Pass and arranged an interview with one of the owners, who did not offer a commitment. Randall had noted serious disadvantages in the area: there was a heavily-traveled railroad line, a maze of power lines, and constant winds. He informed Gabbert that he wished to withdraw his interest in the Pass.

Gabbert had meantime contacted Raymond Cree, former Riverside County Superintendent of Schools, then engaged in the real estate business in Palm Springs. Cree owned acreage in what is now known as Thunderbird Cove, locale of a famous country club and golf course. He assured Randall that he could point out a suitable site there. Randall walked up the bajada as far as Bradley Canyon; his inspection made it clear that expensive terracing would be necessary in order to provide building and parking space, although the area provided privacy, protection from wind, and a favorable visual outlook. Although Cree generously offered a grant of forty acres and a price of only $50 an acre for the remaining quarter-section, Henderson rejected it because of the physical limitations of the terrain.

Cree then suggested that Randall talk with Raymond Wilson, owner of a 160-acre homestead at the junction of Highway 111 and Highway 74, and he arranged a meeting at his Palm Springs office. Wilson was cooperative, and said that he thought a publishing plant with a substantial payroll would be an asset to owners of the area. He offered a twenty-acre site at no cost, and suggested that the owner of an adjoining acreage might offer a similar concession.

Randall's next move was to relocate an old friend, George Schisler, who operated a real estate office in Indio. Schisler owned a half-interest in 160 acres in the cove which later became Palm Desert, and Randall asked for a price quotation.

A month had not yet run out since Randall's military discharge when he consulted his associates in El Centro to report his inquiries and inspections. They agreed that he should choose a site in the cove at the base of the Santa Rosa Mountains. He immediately made a commitment to buy 160 acres of unimproved land from the Henry Jerome Toy estate at $60 an acre. Although he believed the site he had selected was not ideal, he thought it would serve adequately if negotiations failed in deeding an appropriate parcel elsewhere.

Randall's letters at that time made it clear that he believed investment risks were moderate and prospects were excellent in this location. He was well acquainted with the Coachella Valley community and knew that the marketing of dates, grapes, and citrus fruits in the area would require substantial budgets for mail order promotions. The beginnings of substantial investment in hotel, country club, and resort establishments showed great promise. As a veteran printer he knew that the modern equipment he could install at the new location would handle a large volume of printing orders. The commercial stability of Coachella Valley was impressive, and sales effort would be minimized by potential for fast personal service.

While awaiting confirmation from Schisler, Henderson made a tentative effort to explore another possibility. He wrote a letter to the Mollin Investment Company of Los Angeles, which was then selling homesites in a subdivision (Palm Village) on the north side of Highway 111 across from the Wilson homestead.

The letter described the growth of the publishing enterprise in El Centro and the need for larger quarters "in a location essentially recreational and cultural in character, rather than agricultural and commercial." He added that the minimum requirement for his contemplated move would be thirty acres. The editor wrote that he proposed an investment of at least $150,000 in buildings and landscaping, exclusive of equipment and furnishings, and that construction would begin as soon as wartime restrictions on materials and equipment were lifted. Several sites had been considered, he wrote, but he tended to favor the Deep Canyon cove opposite the Palm Village development. He then made a four-point proposal:

That the Company (1) clear title to thirty acres in favor of the *Desert* Magazine corporation, subject to assurances. (2) Provide a domestic water supply, subject to reasonable rates. (3) Erect and equip a post office building. (4) Cooperate in securing a site for an outdoor desert bowl for public use.

In return for these concessions, Henderson suggested several benefits that would accrue to the land owners: (1) Construction of the job-producing plant would begin within six months and occupancy would follow as soon as ready. (2) Already the largest patron of the El Centro post office, the *Desert* Magazine operation would assure the establishment of a post office in the Palm Village area. (3) Travel services and other informational services of the magazine would bring visitors annually to the publication offices, and they would be drawn to the new location. (4) The community surrounding the publishing enterprise would enjoy an enviable cultural prestige.

Randall did not mail this letter. He recalled his brief conversation with his brother Clifford at Accra, and he decided it was time to advise his brother of his progress in site exploration. At this time he had no indication of Cliff's potential interest in investment or development of the desert area. He drove to the Pan Pacific Auditorium, 7600 Beverly Boulevard, Los Angeles, to talk with Cliff and Phil, principal owners and managers of the famous sports and entertainment arena.

Randall read to his brothers the letter he had addressed to the Mollin executives, explained his reasons for the concessions requested, and added that he had not yet mailed the letter. Cliff's response, according to Randall's files, was to ask, "Would you make the same proposal to Phil and me?" "If you fellows really want to get into the real estate business," Randall replied, "I'll make you a better proposal." He then told them about Raymond Wilson's offer of a twenty acre parcel as an inducement to bring the *Desert* Magazine operation to the area. "If you want to come down there and invest in Coachella Valley land, and acquire the Lewis land adjoining Wilson's homestead, I will ask for only twenty acres instead of the thirty acres mentioned in this letter," Randall added.

Cliff and Phil wanted to see maps detailing exact locations of the various sites under consideration. Their interest grew, and they agreed to meet Randall at the desert cove the following weekend. After several days of informational exchanges by telephone, the three brothers met on the land in November 1944. The editor left the meeting with assurances that his brothers would buy the 160-acre Lewis property if Schisler gave a favorable report, and they would deed the twenty acre parcel as requested. The two younger brothers, with long experience and skills in the arts of promotion, apparently saw a rare opportunity during those hours in the sun, because they asked Randall to obtain options on 1620 acres for possible subdivision. Randall worked quietly with brokers and owners for many weeks, often advancing option deposits out of his own pocket, in order to secure the land his brothers wanted. The files contain dozens of letters he wrote in this effort, but there is no evidence that he ever received remuneration of any kind for his work in land acquisition for the P. D. Corporation.

On February 1, 1945, Cliff wrote to Randall: "I will be very anxious to hear any further concerning the 80 acres to the east and the quarter-section adjoining our present 160 acres toward the mountains. These two parcels would complete the picture as far as we are concerned."

The three brothers kept in close touch with each other during the next few months, usually by telephone. They met occasionally at the site to discuss details of their mutual interests. At one of these meetings on the desert they talked about a name that might apply to the proposed new townsite. Randall wanted the word "Desert" to be included, and Phil said, "Why not call it Palm Desert?" The three agreed.

Within four months of the day Randall got out of military uniform, he was ready to turn his thoughts exclusively from land acquisition to the operational requirements of *Desert* Magazine. He wrote to the First Assistant Postmaster General in Washington, informing him of the publishing firm's proposed move to a sparsely populated area that had no postal service, and indicating the volume of postal mailings he expected to handle in the new location. He made personal visits to R. F. Neilson, the district postal inspector at San Bernardino. Neilson later made an official visit to the offices in El Centro to confirm the mailing figures.

Owners of the Palm Village subdivision on the north side of Highway 111 had reportedly pressed their application for a post office to be established on their side of the highway. Col. Robert Ellsworth, then associated with the Mollin Investment Company, visited Randall at El Centro to discuss the matter, and shortly thereafter the Mollin people withdrew their application. Cliff's agreement to provide limited housing for a post office on the south side of the highway was probably a deciding factor. As noted previously, a landmark date was

July 14, 1947, when the new Palm Desert post office opened for business with William Meyers as postmaster.

As plans for the new community took form, Randall often expressed to Cliff his hope that developmental planning would include provisions for cultural facilities in addition to commercial and industrial promotions. He visualized an outdoor amphitheater or natural bowl which would have adequate seating and staging arrangements, sufficient to attract the finest artists and merit loyal audience support. An example he liked to cite was the Ramona Play, a popular annual pageant staged by the people of Hemet Valley.

From the time he began planning *Desert* Magazine's move until his death twenty-five years later, Randall never ceased to press for this type of cultural development, but he never saw it realized in his time. This suggests a strange duality in his character, for he had no talents as a performing artist, he had never worked in theater, and he rarely attended performances. As a business man, he was aware of the need for endowments and other forms of subsidization in order to support permanent community pageants or festivals, but this did not deter him from the idea. In his first walking tours of the Deep Canyon bajada he often pointed out potential sites on the perimeter of the cove which might serve as amphitheaters. In the years that followed he was never able to interest a sponsor or sponsors in promoting construction of an outdoor bowl, although he never lost hope that such a project could be realized through community effort. One of his last letters expressed the hope that an amphitheater might become a reality if it were included in the development plans of the Living Desert Reserve, the College district, or the County Parks and Recreation District.

Cliff agreed in principle with Randall regarding the eventual addition of cultural facilities in community planning, but his primary interest remained in the numerous building projects he had undertaken with the real estate subdivision. Cliff avoided immediate personal commitment when he wrote Randall in February, 1945, suggesting an idea which Randall incorporated in his own building plans:

"Two things come to mind, and they no doubt conform to your long-established plan of development. The project from its inception at the new site should be cast in the public mind as highly cultural, and I believe it would be wonderful to exhibit desert and mountain art, such as the Biltmore Hotel in Los Angeles has at the present time. I think how wonderful it would be to encourage western artists and sculptors to exhibit and even sell their work through a small desert art museum which could be incorporated in your plans. The housing of same could, at least temporarily, be accomplished in the lobby of your building. A desert art museum could be constructed as a future building possibility. This, plus your library of western literature, will make Palm Desert a must for the thousands of regular tourists who visit Palm Springs."

An art gallery became a reality in the spacious outer lobby of the new *Desert* Magazine building. The generous space became the meeting place for numerous pioneer movements: church groups in their formative weeks, first meetings of community library sponsors, land use discussions by leaders of nearby developments, and other community organizations. In due time schools and churches grew out of the sand, a magnificent college campus was built within the community, and a small but attractive public library was created by public subscription: all visible community assets. These cultural assets came about because of the energy and imagination of their sponsors, and because property owners wanted that kind of community. Although, even in the early subdivision days, the area grew rapidly into an affluent community, many civic leaders believed that the time for municipal incorporation and the promotion of major cultural investment should be deferred. The time for realization of Randall's dream of an outdoor amphitheater had not yet come.

Randall's original plan for the publishing building was to establish a desert museum in the foyer, but he was forced to abandon the idea when he learned of the cost of installing and maintaining exhibit cases and employing a curator. He was content later with the art gallery, with open space for early group meetings.

Associated with Cliff and Phil Henderson in the ownership of the Pan Pacific Auditorium were Edgar Bergen, Leonard Firestone, Harold Lloyd, Oscar A. Trippet, William L. Stewart, Jr., and other well-known men in the financial and amusement community of the Los Angeles metropolitan area. Cliff told his associates about investment opportunities in Coachella Valley and invited them to become members of a syndicate for the promotion of these opportunities. They agreed to assist in the financing of surveys, street improvements, water development, and other subdivision costs in the proposed new community. Cliff proudly stated later that in one evening in Leonard Firestone's home a quarter-million dollars was subscribed for these purposes.

For planning and preparation of the townsite plat, Cliff and Phil retained Tommy Tomson, a Henderson brother-in-law and a landscape architect of high reputation in the Los Angeles area. The three men laid out the townsite the way it is today, and their foresight at the beginning solved a problem which now plagues many older cities: the problem of providing adequate parking space for increasing numbers of automobiles.

Early in 1945 Cliff and Phil formed the Palm Desert Corporation to develop the new townsite, a result of agreement with the Pan Pacific backers. The corporation acquired the 160-acre tract adjoining the Raymond Wilson homestead.

That spring Raymond Wilson, Cliff, and Randall met at the site and Wilson and the Palm Desert Corporation agreed to deed twenty acres each to the *Desert* Magazine owners. This provided the forty acres that Randall had originally sought for the publishing enterprise. When the time came for actual deeding, Cliff asked Randall to accept a site about a half-mile east on Highway 111, presumably because the original site would command higher prices for local retail trade; Randall accepted. The editor had to agree that he would not dispose of any of the grant for five years, he would start construction within six months, and would grant appropriate easements for roads and utilities. Since the war freeze on civilian use of building materials had not been lifted at the end of the six-month period, Wilson extended the time for starting construction.

The new corporation launched an ambitious program of development, which included well drilling, street grading and landscaping, sales promotion of residential and commercial frontages, and construction of a luxurious country club.

The Shadow Mountain Club, a major P.D. Corporation project, became a focal center of the new community, and it was soon a popular meeting and eating place. The beautifully landscaped grounds became the setting for an artificial lake, a modern swimming pool, a small golf course, and artfully spaced buildings and cottages. The interior of the main club building had a bar with its own waterfall and a variety of comfortable lobbies and dining rooms. A celebration marked the opening in December 1948, a few weeks after opening of the *Desert* Magazine building.

Phil, third of the four Henderson brothers, died August 1, 1946, in Los Angeles. A strong supporter of the Palm Desert dream, he had an earned reputation as an astute and energetic business man. He was instrumental in the original subdivision planning and he managed the early construction projects. With Phil's passing the burden of townsite management fell on Cliff.

Randall never became a direct participant in the community development project, having neither uncommitted financial resources nor interest in land promotion. He confined himself to his editorial work and planning for the *Desert Magazine* plant and adjacent housing for the staff. Although Randall's advice had been sought in early stages, he and Cliff literally operated in separate worlds, particularly after Randall's retirement in 1958.

Harry O. Davis became a valuable aide in the planning of the magazine enterprise. A retired publication executive with the William Randolph Hearst organization and owner of a date garden just east of the Palm Desert townsite, his expertise in executive management became available to Randall. Davis had been manager of the Panama-California expositions of 1915 and 1935 at San Diego, and he had built and managed the Olympic Village in Los Angeles when the Games were held there in 1932.

Davis, at Randall's request, interviewed architects in Palm Springs to determine who might have appropriate experience with the type of Pueblo design the magazine staff wanted. He recommended Harry Williams and his sons, Stewart and Roger. He then accompanied Henderson on a motor trip to Santa Fe, Taos, and Albuquerque, where they studied details and took pictures of Pueblo construction. Many of the ideas they picked up were incorporated in the building which faces Highway 111, now occupied by the Desert Southwest Art Gallery, Desert Printers, and other tenants.

As mentioned earlier, Randall and I had a voluminous exchange of correspondence before and after his return from military service, and we had discussed in great detail his plans for the magazine's move. I was then an administrative assistant at Merced Army Air Base. Through November and

December 1944 we exchanged letters at least twice weekly, covering the proposed magazine production facilities, space requirements for staff apartments, and a variety of ideas regarding construction and design. My files still contain a set of blueprints I made in October 1944; if my designs eventually proved to be of negative value to the architects, they at least gave Randall and me opportunity for an extended dialog that covered forty-two pages of typing. The point of this personal anecdote is that Randall's ideas about probable building requirements were becoming well fixed before he knew where he would place the structures.

Since gasoline ration coupons were still unavailable, I travelled south by train to walk with Randall in the area of the Raymond Wilson homestead during the weekend of January 6, 1945. We talked more about building plans and he urged me to return to *Desert* Magazine with an interest in the proposed corporation. I had to defer decision because of war manpower restrictions on my civilian employment with the Air Forces, and later in the year my publishing and editing career turned in other directions. My letter rejecting his proposal suggested that I valued his continued friendship more than I valued the prospect of economic gain, and that I doubted that I could invest in a renewed partnership with the same measure of energy and dedication that he had invested. This ended the long exchange in which "we" discussed what "we" would do with "our" enterprise.

During the post-war period essential building materials were in short supply and very expensive. Randall was forced for economic reasons to modify his plans for a basement storage area and central heating-cooling system, and to defer indefinitely his plans for an arts and crafts colony. His cost-plus contract with the R.P. Shea Company of Indio resulted in a total construction cost of $216,000— well above his original estimate. He was able, however, to finance with a mortgage of only $50,000 through the Bank of America at Indio; he frequently expressed his appreciation for the sound financial counsel of Bank Manager Tom Mullan.

Construction started in December 1947. Six months later during the Fourth of July weekend of 1948, the staff, with a well-organized caravan of loaded trucks and cars, was able to move from the El Centro headquarters to the Palm Desert location.

Official opening to the public was set for October 16-17, 1948, although visitors began dropping in soon after occupancy. The open house was well-attended, with special interest centered in the art gallery in the foyer. Probably all visitors who passed through the great main doors glanced up to read the sign,"Friend or Stranger, You Are Welcome Here."

The art gallery provided adequate, well-lighted space for display of the traditional art of the desert southwest. First director of the gallery was J. Marie Ropp of Desert Hot Springs, who had long been associated with the annual Festival of Arts at Laguna Beach. Marie's acquaintance with desert artists and her long residence in the desert country made it possible for her to bring to her displays relevant and exciting examples of talent. When she left after two years she was succeeded by Harriet Day, who had formerly managed the the Desert Inn gallery at Palm Springs. Mrs. Day remained as director until new owners took over the property in 1958. Paula Munson was manager during Shelton's operation. In later years Genevieve K. "Ginger" Neveau and Donald A. Stevning operated the Desert Southwest Art Gallery in the original *Desert* Magazine building, with a growing patronage. An adjoining gem shop in the building has been operated since 1961 by Mr. and Mrs. Harry Cubbage.

Despite higher operating costs because of relative isolation from sources of supply and manpower, the printing-publishing business prospered almost from the beginning of the

Palm Desert experience. Henderson may have found it easy to delegate responsibility to others during his military career, but he found it difficult to do so in his own business. During the first years in the new building he estimated and designed printing orders and supervised their production, took personal interest in accounting, purchasing, and warehousing, helped plan art exhibits, employed personnel, and handled an increasing load of correspondence. His normal work week was 60 to 70 hours. Although he had through the years taken occasional weekends for field trips, he hesitated to extend his trips, even for editorial purposes or for the therapeutic values he attributed to his "feel of the desert."

When Desert Press—the commercial printing operation—gained a reputation for quality production, new customers came to the office. They included Coachella Valley date growers, Palm Springs guest resort operators, and the authors and artists Randall had encouraged over the years.

Growth of printing volume confirmed Randall's early analysis that orders would come from a distance; much of it was conducted on a mail-order basis. It was many years before the town of Palm Desert grew large enough to require much printing; the business never depended on local trade. Revenues from the art gallery came from visitors and tourists, magazine subscriptions came from every state and foreign countries, and book store trade was almost entirely by mail. Randall clearly needed postal service, but the location of a new post office was not vital to his interests. The printing/-publishing operation did not need a town around it; it might have prospered even more had the new subdivision never been created.

Leland Quick, editor of *The Lapidary Journal,* brought his account to Desert Press; he rented office space in the building for several years. He wrote a continuing feature for *Desert* Magazine, "The Amateur Gem Cutter," and his editorial coverage contributed to the increasing interest of "rock hounds."

One of the early customers was Harry Oliver, talented and eccentric desert philosopher of Thousand Palms. A former Oscar-winning Hollywood set designer, Harry chucked the movie business in 1943 to buy a piece of wind-blown sand north of Indio and build an adobe structure he named Fort Oliver. Here he wrote and designed a quarterly publication he called "Harry Oliver's Desert Rat Scrap Book." An assortment of whimsical and humorous short pieces, *Scrap Book* was subtitled "the only newspaper in America you can open in the wind." It was a trial to compose and prove, especially when Harry insisted on hanging around the printshop during the production process. His product was a unique five-page folder printed on heavy paper, sprinkled with droll illustrations out of the ephemora of the past. Now valued as collector's items, copies are prized especially by those who remember Harry's professional talents as founder of the Liar's Club and for his promotion of legends about the lost gold of Peg-Leg Smith. Octogenarian Oliver no longer lives at Thousand Palms, and his family is restoring Fort Oliver as a "historical landmark."

Another promising, but abortive, periodical came to Desert Press from Ernest and Betty Maxwell, who launched the Palm Desert *Progress* and Cathedral *Citizen* in 1951. The young couple had successfully edited and published a newspaper for Idyllwild, and they wanted to extend their operations during the winter season. The eight-page paper they edited was exemplary, but it died an early death from malnutrition.

In June 1952 the first issue of *Archery Magazine*, a monthly publication of the National Field Archery Association, came to Desert Press. Edited by Roy Hoff, it was printed at Palm Desert for several years, until its increasing circulation required the use of high-speed web presses in the city.

The years of hard work and long hours reached a peak in the middle 1950s, but by this time Randall had built an organization of associates with whom he could leave operational details. His letters indicate that he became more and more restive about finding time for work on "The Book," a treatise on sociological and economic problems which had been much on his mind for fifteen years (described in Chapter 10).

He placed the *Desert* Magazine property on the market and in 1958 found a buyer, Charles E. Shelton, a former southern California newspaper publisher. Shelton took over the building, the art gallery, the book store, the printing production facilities, and he retained Randall for the next two years as advisory editor. Randall had reached his 70th birthday, but he had no wish to quit work; he continued regular office hours at his home study until his death.

Five years later Shelton sold the *Desert* Magazine's good will and subscription list to Jack and Coral Pepper, but retained the building and other facilities. Pepper eventually moved the magazine's editorial and circulation offices to a small building on Larrea Street in Palm Desert. William Knyvett is publisher and Jack is editor; the partners announced plans this year to move to larger quarters.

Shelton, after sale of *Desert*, founded the Palm Desert *Post*, a weekly newspaper, with Eugene Conrotto as editor and publisher. The Post now operates from a building near the original *Desert* Magazine plant under the name of Palm Desert Publishing Co., with James Harman as general manager. Desert Printers, now owned by Jaffe and Jaffe, continues to operate in its original location, changing the name of Desert Press.

This chapter has attempted to isolate the publishing and

business aspects of the *Desert* Magazine operation; the next chapter will focus on editorial and literary aspects. It was possible for me to detail the early years in which I was a participant, but I have not attempted to describe subsequent partnerships or the history of incorporation (Desert Press, Inc.) in 1946. But I would like to make an overlapping observation before we pass on to "The Desert Was Our Beat."

Randall edited and published an essentially *personal* magazine, building loyal support through poetry and letters pages and his editorial page of opinion and comment. It is understandable, even implicit, that any change of editors and publishers will alter the tone and structure of any publication. After the War of 1939-45 the tastes of people who turned to the desert for recreation differed widely from the modes and patterns of those who supported Henderson's original editorial credo. The new crop of readers—not necessarily desert residents—liked the uninhibited style of the new writers, and they were attracted to the large four-color photographic pages which became Pepper's regular format.

The first pressrun of *Desert* Magazine was 7,000; twenty-one years later Henderson's last order was for 32,000 copies. Pepper's circulation now tops 50,000. With this growth, it is probable that *Desert* Magazine will survive and prosper into the distant future. But it won't be Randall Henderson's kind of *Desert*—and that's the way it should be.

6. The Desert Was Our Beat

*Beginning with a dream on a
mountaintop, two men launched
Desert Magazine in 1937.*

*The story of Desert Magazine begins with Ol' Breezy.
A relic of the big-wheeled touring model era, Ol' Breezy
had a natural gift for hopping over the rocks and plowing
through the sand of unexplored desert terrain. Ol' Breezy's
metallic bones have long since gone to the junkyard where
aged jalopies eventually find sanctuary, but in the days of
her wheezing career she played a very important part in
the launching of Desert Magazine.*

THIS WAS THE FIRST PARAGRAPH of an article, "Desert's First Eleven Years," which appeared in the November 1948 issue of *Desert* Magazine. It was written by Editor Randall Henderson. Sixteen years later the same writer produced a 19-page chapter for Los Angeles Chapter of the Westerners, Brand Book No. 11, 1964. (A large part of the article, "The Desert Was Our Beat," is reprinted with permission at the end of this chapter). A paragraph expands the theme of the 1925 Chevy noted above:

"I was publishing the daily *Chronicle* at Calexico, California, when I employed Wilson McKenney, a young graduate just out of journalism school. Wilson had an old jalopy, Ol' Breezy he called it, and spent his weekends exploring the desert of the lower Colorado. For each Monday edition of the newspaper he wrote a column about his camping and climbing adventures in out-of-the-way places. His column brought more favorable comment than any other feature of the newspaper. Often I accompanied him on his camping trips and, as we sat around the evening blaze and discussed his desert subjects and reader reaction to them, the thought occurred that we might give readers a whole magazine of it. We envisioned a monthly periodical devoted to the desert, its people, wildlife, arts and crafts, minerals, history, lost mine legends, ghost towns, Indian life and lore, and its travel and recreational opportunities, with photographs and maps, and with as much human interest as we could pack into it..... It was just a dream at first, but gradually, as we camped together in remote canyons where the silence was broken only by our own voices and the occasional call of a coyote, we began to discuss seriously the feasibility of such a publication and the details of its production."

I came to the *Chronicle* on Washington's Birthday, 1930. The Great Depression was beginning to sink its teeth in the country, and I was happy to accept an offer of $18 a week.

That spring and summer I began taking short weekend trips in order to get acquainted with the desert and mountain country surrounding Imperial Valley, and in October I began writing "Little Journeys on the Desert," a column which appeared in print almost weekly for two years. When my employer—twice my age—showed an interest in my weekend activities, I was delighted to have him as a companion. In time Ol' Breezy gasped its last gasp, Randall bought a balloon-tired Model A Ford coupe, and we continued our trips into Baja California, Arizona, and north along the Colorado. His interest began to center in exploration of native palm canyons, an interest which continued for many years.

In June, 1936, Randall and I took a weekend trip to the Santa Rosa Mountains, one of the most memorable of the many exploring trips we took together. We left the highway at Pinyon Flats and drove a rough, narrow, and steep road to the top of Santa Rosa, stopping at Steve Ragsdale's cabin. We camped the night there. I've never seen the stars more brilliant nor felt the air more bracing.

The next morning we walked eastward along the forested ridge, pausing often to marvel at the magnificent panorama of desert and mountains which stretched to the far horizons, north, east, and south. Fortunately, we wore heavy clothing, for although it was typical summer weather in the desert below we were moving above 8,000 feet elevation. We spent the midday hours at the peak, only partly because of the unobstructed views we had of the low lands from Whitewater to Salton Sea. We talked again about starting a magazine, with growing enthusiasm. Our talk ranged from coldly realistic to flights of idealism, from problems of selling advertising space to the values of a poetry page.

Randall said, "Let's sell the *Herald* (we had been co-owners of the Calipatria *Herald* since 1933) and I'll dispose of the *Chronicle*, which will give us limited capital to get started." I agreed. ⋖§ 71 §⋗

We were well aware of the high mortality rate of regional magazines published in the west, but we brushed aside our pessimism in the belief that we knew the desert and its people well enough to produce a publication which would be readable and saleable. Randall would be editor and run the home office; I would be business manager and begin a search for newsstand and advertiser support. What we lacked in capital or future potential we would make up in hard work. It was a grand dream in which we chose to see the fantasy and ignore the suggestion of nightmare.

From where we sat at the peak it seemed possible for us to toss pebbles into the barren desert cove which ten years later became known as Palm Desert. The place had no special significance for us then, but when Randall chose a site for *Desert* Magazine that had to be the place. In his editorial page of August, 1948 (the first issue bearing a Palm Desert address) Randall wrote, "This spot has a sentimental interest for me.....it was during a trip on the ridge overlooking the Palm Desert cove that Wilson McKenney and I more than twelve years ago reached the final decision to launch *Desert* Magazine." He had never forgotten our dream on the mountaintop.

The following spring I closed out my interests in Calipatria, moved my family to El Centro, and took over a desk at the Elite Printing Co., a commercial printing office that provided initial space for the proposed magazine.

At our desert campfires Randall and I had permitted ourselves to become poetic, even prophetic. We would change the prevailing concept that the desert is a desolate and hostile wasteland. We would take our readers behind the grim mask of the arid landscape to the land we had come to know, a land having character and charm only for those who come with understanding. Even then, almost forty years ago, we seemed to know that the health-giving sunshine, night skies studded with diamonds, breezes that bore no poisons, and landscapes of radiant pastels were fragile things that could be destroyed. We wanted our words and pictures to reflect a land of beauty that others might come to know and conserve. Randall prepared a printed dummy of the proposed magazine which contained an editorial, "There Are Two Deserts," which summarized these aspirations— and this became our basic editorial policy.

We had much to do in the first months of 1937; promotion of subscription and advertising commitments, coordination of production schedules, preparation of editorial content. Knowing that our financial resources were limited and must be stretched tight for a long time, Randall and I used pen names in order to reduce author remuneration for our first (November 1937) issue.

Several months before our first deadline Randall wrote to *Writer's Digest,* outlining editorial requirements and inviting free lance writers to submit manuscripts, including short fiction. The response was a deluge of mail. We were appalled at the fictionized versions of wild and woolly days of cowboys, outlaws, gunmen, and vigilantes. It seemed that every writer of radio scenarios with an unsold manuscript in his bottom drawer had shipped it off to *Desert.* We agreed that we did not want this stuff; we wanted to create a different— and we hoped, a more constructive— version of the American West.

Although I wrote a dozen articles for *Desert* during the first months of its publication— and a few more in the early 50s—my active participation in editorial decisions ended when the partnership was terminated in 1939. My correspondence with Randall and observations provided by Lucile Weight (with letters she saved for this use) will serve to illustrate how "Mr. Desert" won his honorary title during his 21 years of editorship.

As circulation grew and readers began to identify with

the philosophy of the magazine, the pile of letters on the editor's desk grew proportionately. For many years he handled all correspondence himself, normally staying at his desk for long work days. He liked to write letters, and he began to think of himself as a teacher or literary coach. There is evidence that he taught well, at least as it related to the effective writing he put in print.

Not all the letters were from aspiring writers; some were from promoters or people who wanted to make a deal. A promotion manager of a swim suit company offered color photographs of movie starlets for the front covers "to modernize and give eye appeal to your magazine." Randall's reply was unusually curt: "Movie celebrities just do not mean a thing to *Desert* Magazine readers. I daresay we would lose half of our circulation overnight if we ran one of your covers. *Desert* and Hollywood are at opposite poles; one is genuine and the other is make-believe."

A subscriber objected to a vacation resort advertisement inserted in the magazine. The editor, switching to his publisher's hat, wrote: "I don't think much of the idea either, but dammit, when we sell a magazine that costs more to print than we receive in subscription price, we have to make up the deficit some way. I have felt that those colored ballyhoo sections were no more objectionable than other forms of advertising. Anyway, there is only one stitch in it and you can yank it out. Please be as tolerant as you can; a $1400 travel ad contract just cancelled out."

A writer offered a story about an Indian woman at a fandango. Randall's courteous letter of rejection included: "The story has a tragic aspect which we try to avoid. We seek to present the more cheerful aspects of the desert, although in this case your story has tremendous human interest."

A woman in New York City wrote that she was writing a book on hiking, and she asked many questions about walking in the desert, where hostels are located, what hazards to avoid, how to identify edible plants. It was a subject close to Randall's heart, and he responded with a three-page letter, concluding with apology that he didn't have time to write the whole chapter.

Articles by Marshal South and the features about Everett Ruess (described later in this chapter) drew a staggering volume of mail. Apparently readers responded emotionally; they wanted to offer opinions or ask questions of a personal nature. Patiently, Randall answered them all.

Never an avid rockhound himself, the editor always had a supply of chalcedony, jade, and other pieces of semi-precious gem material. He would mail off specimens to hobbyists who wanted to exchange, always identifying the place where he found them.

Subscribers wrote that they had overcome their fear of the desert through reading the magazine; some sought employment (and asked the editor's help) so they might have an opportunity to live in the arid land.

Randall's longest letters, sometimes a series of letters, were to novice writers. He never lost patience if he thought a writer would accept advice and if he was an accurate observer with a sense of drama, but had not yet learned how to handle style, viewpoint, or structure, or whatever a writer might need to make readable and interesting copy. He had remarkable success in urging neophytes toward competence in the craft. Some letter writers obviously had little or no schooling, but had "educated" powers of observation and narration. These were the most difficult for the editor to manage because such leads required followup; he could not afford to send an associate editor for interview, photography, and skilled writing. It pained him when he didn't have the resources (usually meaning his own time) to follow up on all the "good tips."

During the war, when Lucile was acting editor, letters were often poignant. Readers who were literally shut-ins because of restrictions on tires and gasoline found therapy and solace for deprivation through the magazine. Some expressed their feeling that "*Desert* is something to hold on to in times like these." Long handwritten letters came from soldiers and sailors in all parts of the world; some sent gems, shells, camp newspapers, something to share with someone they knew would react with understanding.

The remainder of this chapter will appear in first person— Randall's words— as they appeared in Westerner's Brand Book No. 11, 1964. Selected portions— bearing the same title as that used for this chapter— are reprinted here with permission of the Brand Book editor.

The mail brought letters of inquiry from writers who later became regular contributors, men and women who were qualified to write authoritative material on many aspects of past and contemporary life on the desert. Bylines which appeared frequently in the early issues of *Desert* included those of Arthur Woodward, then curator of history at the Los Angeles County Museum; Lon Garrison, then a park ranger in Death Valley National Monument; Mrs. White Mountain Smith, wife of the superintendent of Petrified Forest National Monument; John Hilton, the desert artist; Charles Kelley, historian of Utah; John D. Mitchell, dean of the lost mine authorities; Walter Ford, a school teacher in San Diego; and a little later, Jerry Laudermilk of Pomona College and Nell Murbarger, the roaming reporter of the desert. Occasionally we got a manuscript from Barry Goldwater of Phoenix, whose father once had a trading post at old Ehrenberg.

During the first year of publication we received no fiction we felt worthy of our pages. The only exception to this was Lon Garrison's tall tales of Hard Rock Shorty, a fictitious old jackass prospector of his own creation. During the second year of publication I mentioned casually on the editorial page that we still planned to use fiction as soon as we could get suitable material. But readers did not want it. The fan mail brought so many protests that we gave up the idea.

From an editorial standpoint, our first lucky strike was Norton Allen, the artist. Norton was an amateur archeologist whose hobby was tramping the desert in quest of old Indian sites— until an illness left him so crippled he could walk only with crutches. He was a fine cartographer with a thorough knowledge of desert geography.

Norton worked at his home in La Mesa, California, or in a trailer when he was on camping trips with his parents. He knew the desert so well that when errors occurred in the instructions from which he was working, he would correct them. I dare say that during the 21 years I was at the editor's desk and since then, for he continues to draw maps for *Desert's* present publishers, literally millions of motorists and hikers have found their way unerringly to the destinations he mapped for them.

Most controversial writer was Marshal South of Ghost Mountain in San Diego County. Marshal had once served as an officer in the British army. He came to the United States after World War I and hoped to win a place for himself as a writer and dramatist in Hollywood.

But he was a non-conformist whose radical views often antagonized associates who might have helped him. During the 1920s he made a meager living at various odd assignments. Then the Great Depression came and he became a private in the army of the unemployed.

Marshal became a rebel against a society which could not provide work for its people. He persuaded his bride, Tanya, to share a great adventure with him. They would turn their backs on civilization and go out on the desert and live as did the Indians of this region before the white man came.

They took off from a coastal city in an old jalopy and headed into the mountainous back country of San Diego County. They followed the unbeaten trails, and late one afternoon came to the base of a low range of mountains overlooking the old Vallecito stage station of the Butterfield days. They climbed to the top of the ridge above with their blankets, spread a tarpaulin between two juniper trees, and camped there for the night.

This was in the early 1930s, and this mountaintop remained their home until Marshal's death in 1948. There was neither shelter nor water at the top of Ghost Mountain— the name they gave their retreat— but they built a crude camp with the materials at hand and carried their water from a spring at the base of the hill. In the years following they built a comfortable adobe house, and later a cistern in which to store the water which drained from the roof of the house.

The water for the adobes, cement, roofing, materials for doors and windows, building hardware, and crude furniture were all packed up the steep hillside to the site. They cultivated the friendship of their wildlife neighbors— kit foxes, rabbits, reptiles, chipmunks, rodents. All life on the mountain was sacred to them.

Occasionally Marshal would make a trip out to Julian for salt, sugar, flour, coffee, and seasoning, but they sought always to harvest their food from the desert and nearby mountains as prehistoric Indians had done. They learned to roast the buds of the mescal or agave. They gathered acorns, pinyon nuts, and mesquite beans and harvested what seed they could from the chia sage. After the cistern was completed and the winter rains came, they were able to grow a little garden with water they drew from the well.

Three children were born during their sojourn at the home which they named Yaquitepec. As the time approached for the arrival of each of the children Marshal would take Tanya out to a hospital in the nearest coastal town for proper medical care.

My first acquaintance with the Souths was in 1939 when the *Saturday Evening Post* carried a feature story written by Marshal, giving many details of their experiment in primitive living. The *Post* article was vague as to the location of Ghost Mountain, and I wanted to get the mailing address. Here was a writer who was a natural for *Desert* Magazine. My quest for clues to the location of Ghost Mountain and its nearest post office came to an unexpected and happy ending when I received a letter from Marshal asking if he might write something for *Desert*. Of course the answer was yes, and I asked for directions so I might go to Yaquitepec and discuss some ideas I had in mind. This was in late 1939. The adobe house was not yet completed, but the Souths were occupying it, and at the end of a well-concealed trail to the top of the mountain I found two healthy youngsters scampering among the rocks, a neat motherly woman weaving a basket, and Marshal excavating the hole which was to be the cistern. Here was an intelligent American family imposing upon themselves disciplines which few civilized people would endure, but wholesome and happy. The reward for their self-exile was a degree of independence which few Americans know, and for which fewer would pay the price.

They told about their plans for the future— the garden they would grow when there was water in the cistern, the outdoor fireplace, exploratory expeditions into the surrounding desert in search for ancient Indian campsites, and for seeds and herbs which would add to their food supply. Theirs was a busy life, but it was never drudgery because tomorrow's dreams would make Yaquitepec more habitable. They had goals— and enthusiasm. They were sustained by a faith that held the promise of better days ahead.

During my two hours on the mountaintop, it was arranged that Marshal would become a regular writer for *Desert*. During 1940 he would write a serial— a monthly diary of life at Yaquitepec, detailing the problems and satis-factions of their lonely existence on a remote desert mountain.

Marshal wrote well, and soon the readers of *Desert* were sharing with Tanya and Rider and Rudyard the thrills which every rising sun brought to this little family. We were receiv-ing an increasing volume of fan mail. *Desert* readers were interested, but by no means in accord. Some of them admired the courage of Tanya and Marshal and regarded their exper-ience as a noble experiment in human adventure. Others fretted about the lack of schooling for the children and were apprehensive that, growing up in this isolated environment, they would be misfits in the society to which they must return eventually.

But the readers need not have worried. Tanya was a fine teacher and, following Marshal's death in 1948, she moved to a coastal city where the children entered school well advanced in their studies and readily adapted themselves to the social complex of community life. One of the teachers once wrote that Victoria, youngest of the three children, was the brightest and prettiest girl in the senior class at high school.

Since desert history was to have an important place in our editorial coverage, I was delighted when I received a letter from Arthur Woodward of the Los Angeles County Museum. He suggested some historical subjects on which he had done research. For ten years he was a regular contri-butor to *Desert*. I soon gained a high regard for the range and accuracy of his historical reports. At various times he recalled for our readers the story of old Fort Mojave, the reclamation of Palo Verde Valley by Thomas Blythe, early day steamboating on the Colorado River, the explorations of Father Kino, the founding of old Ehrenberg, and scores of other courageous and sometimes tragic episodes in man's conquest of the desert Southwest.

Arthur was also an archeologist, and one summer he

invited me to spend a month with him locating and recording with photographs and sketches some of the best preserved petroglyphs and pictographs left by ancient tribesmen on thousands of rocks scattered over the Southwest. Our trek included parts of Colorado, New Mexico, Utah, and Arizona. The petroglyphs, incised in the rock faces with stone tools, are still very sharp and clear in some instances. The pictographs, painted on the rocks with pigments and preservatives known only to the tribesmen, have retained their form and color only in caves and sheltered places.

It was easy to identify some of the glyphs— the coyote, the sun, rain, reptiles, and other symbols representing wildlife or the natural elements. Arthur hoped that by comparative studies of widely scattered examples of this prehistoric art it might be possible to deduce patterns which would give significance to this phase of Indian culture.

This probably was the most intensive study ever made of this subject. And yet, a year later when I asked him what his research had revealed, he replied: "I do not know yet whether those glyphs express the artistry of tribal poets, the wisdom of the medicine men, or the doodlings of aboriginal morons."

Indian life and lore had an important place in the editorial formula of *Desert* during the years I occupied the desk. I had spent some months among the Chemehuevis and Mojaves of the Colorado River country soon after leaving school, and it was my good fortune to enlist the cooperation of two writers especially well qualified to interpret the life and culture of the tribesmen.

Mrs. White Mountain (Margie) Smith, whose husband was then superintendent of the Petrified Forest Monument in Arizona, had spent many months on the Hopi reservation in northern Arizona. She was very fond of these people and knew the intimate details of their religion and home life. I had the privilege in August, 1938, of accompanying Mrs.

Smith and White Mountain to the annual Hopi snake dances. It is a deeply religious ceremony, and as I came to know these people as revealed to me by Mrs. Smith, I gained a deep respect for them.

Their reservation is surrounded by the lands of the Navajo— but the two peoples are as different in many respects as the Eskimos differ from the Fiji Islanders. The Hopis are shrewd traders, and the story is told about one of their tribesmen going into the Navajo reservation one day with a basket of peaches and returning that evening with a Navajo pony.

While Mrs. Smith wrote knowingly about the Hopi Indians, and also contributed interesting personality copy about some of the white traders on the reservations, the Navajo also had a loyal friend on our staff of free lancers in the person of Richard Van Valkenburg. Van was an ethnologist in the service of the U.S. Indian Bureau, stationed at Ft. Defiance, then the Bureau headquarters on the Navajo reservation.

He and Mrs. Smith often met each other as they traversed the Indian country— and they would invariably engage in a friendly argument as to the comparative virtues of the Navajo and Hopi. I believe it was Mrs. Smith who first suggested to Van that he submit copy to *Desert* Magazine.

His first manuscript recounting an interesting episode in Navajo history was a welcome subject. But Van had never written for the press and his narrative was strangled with meaningless detail. Here was a writer worth cultivating, for he had access to the historical records of the largest and most colorful tribe in North America. He was learning their language, knew them well, and had their respect.

Van was eager to be a writer, and I was confident he had the talent and the material to write acceptable copy for our readers. After much correspondence his initial article was revised to meet our standards. His next effort was better, but further coaching would be necessary.

He wrote me that a Navajo medicine man had reported the discovery of an ancient cliff dwelling in a remote canyon on the reservation. The Indian was unable to scale the cliff to reach the mud-and-stone dwelling, but the walls seemed well preserved and well decorated with three large pictographs of wild turkeys.

I had planned to take a trip into the Indian country within a few weeks and asked him to wait and let me accompany him to the ruins. On the hike to the canyon we camped overnight at the hogan of the medicine man who was to be our guide, and our host butchered a lamb that evening as a special treat for his guests.

Next day we reached the prehistoric dwellings, but the sandstone cliffs had eroded to such an extent we were unable to follow the finger and toe steps which the ancient dwellers had used to reach their dwelling in a recess far up the sidewall. The three turkeys were a conspicuous landmark, well preserved in black and white pigment.

Much of our two-day trek together was spent in suggesting to Van how this story should be written. He was an apt pupil, and after that his stories required very little editing. He became one of our most popular writers until 1952 when he was stricken with a heart attack. The Navajos gave him a burial ritual worthy of a tribal chieftain.

The mail was bringing increasing numbers of manuscripts from free lance writers as *Desert* became better known. But hardly one in twenty of them was acceptable material. Too many of them were tainted with the tenderfoot image of the desert— a land swarming with rattlesnakes and venomous insects, of untamed Indians and gun-toting frontiersmen, a land of intolerable heat from which there was no escape, of lone prospectors with burros panning the sands for yet undiscovered gold, and of cactus storing an ever-ready supply of water for the thirsty traveler. Also there were scholarly essays, very correct, but without a spark of human interest. Gradually, we became convinced that it would be easier to make writers of desert people than to instil the feel of the desert into professional writers whose manuscripts were plotted in the more sophisticated regions beyond the far horizons. Once I wrote to a woman whom I knew quite well, but who had only a casual acquaintance with this arid land: "If you want to write for *Desert* you should move out here and stay long enough to get some sand in your hair and some cactus spines in your shirt tail." Fortunately she had a sense of humor— and we remained friends.

In my role as literary coach, one of my most apt pupils was John Hilton, now recognized as one of the West's finest landscape artists. John is a very versatile fellow. He is a botanist specializing in cactus, a gem collector and lapidary, and an entertaining musician. He was then residing at his little art and gem shop on Highway 99, fourteen miles south of Indio. He had seen the first issue of *Desert* at the Valerie Jean date shop across the road, and he drove to El Centro to query the possibility of becoming a contributor.

John was well acquainted with the semi-precious gem and mineral fields in the California and Arizona deserts, and he suggested writing a monthly travelog for the rockhounds.

Here was another natural for *Desert*, and for eight years Hilton wrote about field trips, with maps by Norton Allen, for nearly every issue of the magazine, except during the war years when there was no gas for field tripping. He alternated occasionally with biographical sketches of desert artists with whom he had a wide acquaintance. His subjects included Jimmy Swinnerton, Clyde Forsythe, Paul Lauritz, Burt Proctor, William Krehm, George Frederick, Fritioff Persson and many others.

John's first manuscript was an editor's nightmare. But I

was not dismayed, for it revealed a real sense of drama which is a feature writer's most important asset. I was sure he would develop the technical skill to make a good reporter, and my confidence was well justified. John has the knack of seeing the drama in every situation, and he soon added a very readable writing style to his other achievements.

During the first few months when the mail failed to bring enough suitable material for the next issue, Wilson McKenney and I would fill in the gap. For some issues, he and I would write two or three feature articles, using pen-names for by-lines.

Nell Murbarger became a contributor to *Desert* in August, 1949, when her first manuscript— featuring the ghost mining camp of Shakespeare, New Mexico— won instant acceptance. In the following years she became a regular and popular contributor to our pages.

Like many other magazine writers, Nell began her journalistic career on a country newspaper. But towns— and even cities— were too small for the gypsy spirit of this young lady who had grown up on the midwestern plains made famous by Wild Bill Hickok, Calamity Jane, and Deadwood Dick. She gave up a promising newspaper career to roam over the western country and write magazine articles about its history, frontier characters, ghost towns, landmarks— and always about people. Her special interest has been the abandoned mining camps. She travels alone much of the time and camps wherever she happens to be when the sun goes down.

Nell is a master of the art of portraying human character and eccentricities. She invariably finds a lone survivor or two in the vicinity of each gold camp, and these become the actors in history that otherwise might be dull and statistical. She has written three books about the ghost camps in the desert Southwest, the latest being *Ghosts of the Adobe Walls* in which she has brought life and interest to the abandoned ruins of mining and prehistoric Indian occupation of Arizona. This volume was published in 1964 at Paul Bailey's Westernlore Press.

Nell and her mother have spent the last four winters on gypsy tours in Mexico and Central America. They travel in a camper and much of the time they follow the back roads to remote settlements where life is still very primitive. She loves to write about people. Her book, *30,000 Miles in Mexico,* is a day-to-day record of one of these trips.

Artists and poets have played an important role in dispelling the image of the desert as a grim and desolate wasteland. Everett Ruess was one of these. His name, like woodsmoke, conjures far horizons and mystery.

Everett left Kayenta, Arizona, November 11, 1934, to write, paint, and explore some of the ancient cliff dwellings of the canyon country in Arizona and Utah. His last letters to his parents in Los Angeles stated that he would be unable to communicate with them for ten weeks. Alone with his paints, books, and burros, he disappeared into what at that time was the most uninhabited region of the United States. He never returned.

Poet, artist, and adventurer, the desert trails were his roads to romance. His paintings captured the black-shadowed desolation of aboriginal homes high up in the recesses of the cliff walls. His poetry told of beauty and wind, and the artifacts of prehistoric people. He sang of the wasteland's moods. Everett belonged to the desert, and in the end it claimed him.

I first learned about the saga of Everett Ruess in early 1938, soon after *Desert* Magazine appeared on the newsstands. Hugh Lacy, a Los Angeles writer, sent a letter of inquiry in which he outlined briefly the strange gypsy life of a young man who for four years had wandered the desert wilderness and then dropped from sight. The story, Lacy wrote, would be written serially in the notes and letters and poetry Everett had written to family and friends during his nomad life in the wilderness.

This would be welcome copy for the pages of *Desert*, for it would give the readers a glimpse of arid America through the eyes of an intelligent young man who had written: "I prefer the saddle to the street car and the star-spangled sky unknown to any paved highway, and the deep peace of the wild to the discontent bred in cities."

Hugh Lacy's stories of Everett Ruess appeared serially through 1939, and later we published them in book form with the title *On Desert Trails With Everett Ruess*.

Everett's last journey was into the canyon country along the Colorado River east of Escalante, Utah. When they failed to hear from him after a few weeks, his parents spread the alarm, and search posses spent weeks combing the region of his last known campsite. They found his two burros in an improvised corral along Davis Creek, a tributary of the Escalante River, but no trace of Everett or his bedroll, artists' supplies or notes ever came to light. In my book *On Desert Trails Today and Yesterday*, I wrote what I have always regarded as the most plausible explanation of his disappearance— that he probably met death at the hands of cattle rustlers operating in the area, who suspected him of being an agent of the law, seeking evidence which would incriminate them. But there is no confirmation of this. As water rises in the new Lake Powell being formed behind Glen Canyon dam, the region of Everett's last camp will be inundated and likely clues to the mystery will be forever lost.

During my years as editor and reporter for *Desert* I spent as much time as possible in the field. With a competent staff in the office, it was possible to be absent for as long as a month at a time. These trips gave me contact not only with those who were writing for our pages, but also personal acquaintance with many rugged men and women who were playing leading, though often obscure, roles in the heroic drama being enacted on the desert stage of this period.

Just to mention a few of them: Harry Goulding and his wife Mike, veteran Indian traders in Monument Valley; Bill and Katherine Wilson at Rainbow Lodge, of which Barry Goldwater of Arizona was a part owner at that time; Cozy McSparron, colorful trader of Canyon de Chelly; Shine Smith, the big-hearted free lance missionary on the Navajo reservation, loved by Indians and whites alike; Chee Dodge, for many years the stalwart chief of the Navajo; Art Greene, lodge-keeper and boatman, who now has a Park Service boat concession on Lake Powell; Desert Steve Ragsdale of the Chuckawalla Valley in California; Ross Musselman, veteran guide on Utah trails; Death Valley Scotty and Ray Goodman, former superintendent of Death Valley National Monument; Nellie Coffman of Palm Springs; John and Louisa Wetherill, Indian traders at Kayenta; Charlie Brown, state senator from Shoshone; Dr. Clarence Salsbury of the Ganada mission in the Navajo country— the list could go on and on.

N Allen

7. Where Wild Palms Grow

*Washingtonia fan palm is one of the desert's
most beautiful native trees; its habitat
includes canyons of Palm Desert cove.*

*During a quarter century of exploring the palm can-
yons of the desert, Randall Henderson wrote and published 30 or more definitive articles for* Desert *on this
subject. He gained a reputation as the leading desert palm
authority of his time, and was the first to publicize the
locations and range of Washingtonia. Nine of his graphic
descriptions (April 1938 to March 1956) covered the
canyons of the Palm Desert bowl. Most of his palm articles
appeared before 1945, because by that time he was 57
years old and he had nearly exhausted the potential for*

field study. I walked and climbed with Randall on seven of these cove excursions, and I can vouch for the accuracy of the accounts given below, which have been drawn— with minor editing—from his notes and unfinished manuscript. The concluding narrative in this chapter is quoted directly from one of his earliest accounts.

PALM DESERT is a name truly descriptive of the cove community at the base of California's Santa Rosa mountain range. For here, radiating from the perimeter of this sheltered cove, are seven canyons in which the fan palm *Washingtonia filifera* is growing wild in its native habitat.

The native palm must not be confused with the six varieties of date palm which are commercially grown on the floor of Coachella Valley and which produce marketable fruit. Origin of the *Washingtonia* has not been determined by scientists, but they agree it is uniquely indigenous to the eastern (watered) canyons of the ranges south from the San Bernardinos into northern Baja California. Varieties found in northern Africa and other arid regions of the world do not identify with the southern California species. Date palms were originally imported from the gardens which border the Mediterranean Sea, and the local fruit is famed around the civilized world because of its careful cultivation and cross-breeding.

Randall saw his first fan palms in 1921, and for many years exploration of desert canyons in search of wild palm groups was his consuming hobby. Over the years he logged 87 separate oases in the canyons and foothills of Riverside, San Bernardino, San Diego, and Imperial counties— and many more in Baja California. He estimated that there were at least 11,000 native palms in the southern California desert, approximately half of them in Riverside County— and the number increased during his observations.

Expanding subdivisions created by increasing numbers of metropolitan dwellers who seek retirement homes in the desert community have caused the phasing out of many date palm gardens from La Quinta to Indio. But Randall credited the work of the U.S. Bureau of Land Management, a growing awareness of ecological values, and the natural processes of plant proliferation with the fact that the wild palms in their relatively isolated canyons are increasing in numbers.

There are 34 fan palm groups in the canyons on the perimeter of Coachella Valley, living at elevations from the valley floor to 3200 feet. The most famous, of course, is Palm Canyon, a few miles south of Palm Springs and just over the ridge west of Palm Desert. There an estimated 3000 native trees grow along a seven-mile sector of the lower gorge, and their rugged beauty draws thousands of visitors annually.

Henderson's initial acquaintance with the native palms of this area was in the early 30's when he drove down the winding Palms-to-Pines highway and stopped at a roadside cabin about halfway down the grade. There was no response when he knocked on the door, but he noticed a crudely lettered sign on the lean-to porch: WELCOME TO HIDDEN PALMS. RELAX AND FORGET THE WORLD. ENJOY YOURSELF. NOTHING FOR SALE.

Following a rock-rimmed trail that led to a hilltop beyond the cabin, he reached a point where he could look down on a stately group of palms in a narrow canyon. The path leading into the gorge seemed to invite exploration. When he reached the palms, he found a spring of good water surrounded by the tracks of bighorn sheep.

On later visits to the cabin he became acquainted with Virgil Adair, the owner. From him he learned that there were wild palms in nearly all the canyons in the area. Adair worked a nearby feldspar claim, he had appointed himself guardian of the palm oasis, and visited the palms daily to obtain his water supply. He has long since passed away, and the cabin is now used by Buddy Rose, a Palm Desert gardener.

A few years ago Randall counted 55 palms in the group. Although this oasis is within 100 yards of the highway (State Route 74), the trees are not visible from the pavement. Hundreds of motorists pass daily without knowing that, concealed only a few paces away, is one of the loveliest palm oases in the Colorado Desert.

In the years after his Hidden Palms visit, Henderson explored other canyons in the area and in time his log book contained notes on seven main and tributary canyons which drain into the Palm Desert cove. In addition there is a palm oasis along Bear Creek on the north slope of Sheep Mountain above La Quinta, and there are many natives of the palm family in Magnesia Spring Canyon which drains into Rancho Mirage cove to the west. The editor's notes describe the seven oases of the Palm Desert cove, all of which are within ten miles of the settled community:

CAT CREEK PALMS: The location of Cat Creek may be identified by the dry watercourse which crosses Section 36 on the west side of Highway 74— the Section now occupied by five-acre "jackrabbit" homesteaders. Homesteaders have built cabins, some very attractive cottages, which nestle into the slopes and hilltops of the mile-square area. The dry course of Cat Creek cuts through the Section and crosses the highway, but farther up where the mountains close in to form a rocky gorge there are a few streams of flowing water with waterfalls and crystal-clear pools.

The creek grade rises steadily as it enters the mountain slope. Randall wrote, "As I neared the creek source on the side of Haystack Mountain I came upon one of the most gorgeous groups of native palms I have ever found in any canyon. I counted 78 trees in the cluster, but I am not sure the count is accurate because identifying individuals in such a minia-

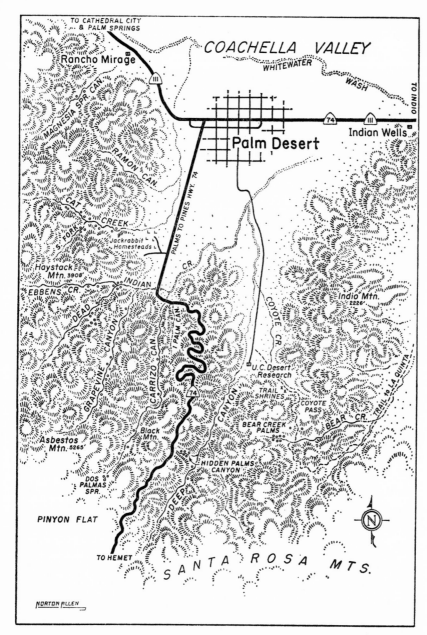

There are seven palm canyons located in the perimeter of the Palm Desert cove; many others may be found in nearby mountain slopes. This map by Norton Allen, the artist who drew the illustrations for chapter headings, is reproduced with permission from *Desert* Magazine, March, 1965.

ture jungle is not a mathematical certainty. I am certain, however, that I shall remember the beauty of this group long after the figures are forgotten."

A distinctive characteristic of this group is the wide range of ages among the living specimens. There are the bare trunks of ancient trees bearing the char of old lightning-caused fires, and beside them are full-skirted giants. Crowding toward the sunlight are many young palms, struggling for existence in a favorable environment.

"The oasis I have described is the uppermost habitat of the palm in this canyon. I continued for half a mile, and the higher I climbed the more impressive was the mountain scenery. I reached a ridge where I could look down into the branches of the upper canyon. Then I looked up, and silhouetted against the sky was a mountain ram, his head so turned that the curve of his horns was sharp against the blue sky. He stood like a statue, watching me, perhaps a quarter mile away. We gazed at each other for minutes, then he dropped out of sight, followed by a ewe. The picture was reward enough for six hours of strenuous climbing."

There is no trail up Cat Canyon; one simply follows the streambed, picking the least formidable route around boulders. The trip requires a lot of scrambling over jumbled masses of rock and smooth-ground waterfalls.

DEAD INDIAN CREEK: On the Palm Desert quadrangle map it is identified as "Dead Indian Creek," but neither the Indian's name nor the reason for his demise is recorded in local history. The "creek" is visible only when flood waters surge down the mountain on rare occasions, sometimes filling the dry stream bed with a raging torrent.

Motorists departing from Palm Desert on Highway 74 cross two bridges where the paved road leaves the floor of the desert to start its winding ascent of the Santa Rosa mountain slope. The first of these bridges spans Dead Indian Creek, and is the starting point for hikers who want to visit this rocky gorge. Although the dry sandy arroyo may be traversed in a four-wheel-drive vehicle, travel on foot or on horseback is recommended. Within a half-mile, walking will be necessary anyway.

On arriving at the oasis, not visible from the highway, the hiker will find a group of 22 wild palms so closely huddled together that penetration is difficult. The creekbed appears to end at this point, but there's more ahead. Scaling a precipitous dry waterfall to the right, one finds himself in the Ebbens Creek tributary.

The main channel of Dead Indian Creek continues to the left of the 22-palm oasis. Climbing a steep talus slope, the hiker finds a well-defined channel in which there are pools of water at intervals. At the waterholes are occasional small groups of palms, and there is evidence that bighorn sheep frequently visit the place.

Upper Dead Indian canyon is a precipitous gorge, and the hiker must often detour dry waterfalls. On the slopes above the creekbed are the remains of old Indian trails. At one point near the headwaters of the creek rocks are piled in great monuments, as though an ancient race of giants had staked out claims, marking corners with huge slabs too heavy to be lifted by ordinary mortals.

EBBENS CREEK: The Ebbens Creek tributary is a lovely palm canyon. After the hiker scales the steep waterfall above the 22-palm oasis the traverse is not as rugged as Dead Indian Creek.

The creek takes its name from Theodore Ebbens, a prospector who tramped these mountains with his burro late in the last century. One of his eccentricities was to collect frying pans for his camping outfit. It was said of him that whenever he set up a new camp his first chore was to nail a long cross-piece to a tree, on which he hung up his array of skillets.

In a brief sketch about the old prospector written by Dr. Edmund Jaeger for *Desert* Magazine in 1956 appears this description: "Ebbens Creek, which is really no creek at all but only an open and shallow scenic gulley, is a little tough going at times, but the scenic views of the distant desert and the beautiful gardens filled with agave and ocotillo made us forget our exertions. Most exciting of all was the finding of numerous spoor of the desert bighorn, and finally seeing two fine adult rams accompanied by an ewe..... In Ebbens Creek canyon we saw a splendid group of *Washingtonia* palms, full-fronded to the base and unspoiled by fire vandals.

"In the spring season this must have been a fine locus for the Ebbens camp, for then the group of palms is surrounded by a glorious garden of flowering annuals and blossoming shrubs. At that time, too, the place was probably the source of a tiny streamlet which could be heard tinkling its way over the rocks and meandering languidly down the clean, sandy, flower-bordered wash.

"When the government surveyors worked on the map of the Santa Rosa mountains, they hired Ebbens to pack in supplies for them. He knew that country like a book, and was a valuable guide. I think they liked old Ebbens. Anyway, they named one of his old hang-outs after him, and that is how his name got on the map."

GRAPEVINE CREEK: Another tributary of Dead Indian Creek is Grapevine Creek, a precipitous gorge which can be ascended only by rock-climbers equipped with rope and pitons. After trying most of one day in 1947 to make his way up the creekbed, Henderson had to give up, but returned later with two companions. They worked *downward*, using rope to rapel over the dry waterfalls.

The three men started from The Tors, then the mountain home of Nina Paul Shumway and now the retreat of the artist, Frances Rich. The water supply at The Tors comes from a spring at the headwaters of Grapevine Creek on Asbestos Mountain, at 4000-foot elevation.

At 3000 feet they reached the first of several palm groups which grow along the creek. The area supports vegetation of the Upper Sonoran zone; specimens included Rhus ovata, wild apricot, nolina, juniper, yucca, catsclaw, ephedra, jojoba— a striking variety rivalled in few botanical gardens.

Moving down the canyon, the men counted 101 wild palms over three feet in height, and there were many pools of water but no stream.

They roped down over a 30-foot waterfall— rapelling is the word used by rock-climbers— a simple exercise and quite safe when the proper technique is used. The method is to double the rope, place the loop around a solid tree or rock (the belay) and descend in a self-manipulated sling. The limitations of this technique are the length of rope and the availability of safe belays. The climber, on reaching the terminus of his descent, has only to pull one strand of the rope in order to retrieve his equipment. The normal practice in a party of two or more is for the first climber over the edge to descend unencumbered, and he waits to unfasten packs which are eased down to him. The first time over the brink may be a critical test for the novice, but after he learns to trust the rope and the strength of his wrists, the experience can become a thrilling sport.

Grapevine is too inaccessible to become well-known among the scenic canyons of the Palm Desert area. Some conservationists have expressed apprehension lest the growing popularity of the desert as a recreational area will result in the destruction of the environmental quality of the canyons in this area. Henderson's notes conclude with the hope that the isolation of many charming canyons (due to natural hazards of entry) will remain a protective barrier against their despoliation. "Fortunately, the dunderheads who paint their names on the rocks and scatter tin cans over the landscape do not penetrate this kind of wilderness terrain."

CARRIZO CREEK: Following around the perimeter of Palm Desert cove in a counter-clockwise direction, the next wild palms are found at Dos Palmas, a historic watering-place at the headwaters of Carrizo Creek.

The spring at Dos Palmas long ago ceased flowing, according to some geologists, probably due to the faulting of foundation structures by earthquakes. One of the original palms has died, probably due to lack of water, but the trunk remained standing a few years ago. A replacement has grown about 50 feet downstream, so the landmark is still "two palms." These palms grow at an elevation of 3500 feet, the highest *Washingtonia* to be found in its native habitat.

"From this tiny oasis I trekked the length of the canyon to the desert floor in 1945, and found only five other wild palms growing along the way. Nearing the lower sector of the canyon, my way was blocked by an almost vertical pitch of dry waterfall. Since I had no rope for rapelling, I climbed out of the canyon and detoured in a small tributary parallel to the Palms-to-Pines highway. In the short distance before I reached the floor of the cove, I found only one small *Washingtonia*. Since this little drainage channel had no name, I entered it in my log-book as "One Palm Canyon."

"On that first visit to Dos Palmas early on a September morning I heard the call of a canyon wren. There is no note, or series of notes, quite like the descending scale of this bird of the desert wild lands. I share the feeling of William Leon Dawson when he wrote 'Heard across the wastes of chapparal, or in the cool depths of some rugged ravine, this song of the canyon wren is at once the most stirring and imaginative, the most delightful which the wilderness of California has to offer.'

"For the guidance of those who would like to visit this old watering place (now dry), here is my log: Drive up Highway 111, turn right on the blacktop Pinyon Crest road. Continue on this road seven-tenths of a mile to a little sign, 'Dos Palmas, ½ mile.' Turn right on the ungraded dirt road, and at three-tenths of a mile is a parking place overlooking the two palm trees."

U.S. Forestry rangers have placed a picnic table at Dos Palmas, but it is seldom used. The 100-yard distance from the parked car is a steep and rocky mountain slope thick with chaparral. A traverse of Carrizo Creek is a field day for those who like rough and rocky hiking. The upper canyon offers an inviting adventure for botany students of the Upper Sonoran zone.

HIDDEN PALMS OASIS: The foregoing paragraphs describe briefly the five wild palm canyons in the perimeter of Palm Desert cove which lie west of Highway 74. On the east side of the highway are two rocky gorges where *Washingtonia* also live.

One of the most accessible of all the palm groups— and yet one seldom seen by the motorist speeding along the highway— is Hidden Palms oasis. It lies in a rugged tributary of Deep Canyon gorge within a stone's throw of Highway 74. This is the oasis referred to at the beginning of this chapter, as seen from the top of the hill back of the Adair cabin, 10.6 miles from Palm Desert on Highway 74.

Twenty-five years ago there were 55 mature trees growing around a spring of good water at this place. The spring, like many other former watering places on the Santa Rosa range, has ceased to flow in recent years, but the trees seem to have adequate moisture at their roots for survival.

DEEP CANYON ADVENTURE: The great gorge which drops away so precipitously on the east side of the Palms-to-Pines highway as it winds down the north slope of the Santa Rosas to Palm Desert cove is identified on the maps as Deep Canyon — and deep it is. This gorge is the habitat of a few wild palms, but not many. Cloudburst torrents which surge down between the narrow walls of this flood channel at intervals are too powerful to permit the growth of obstructing trees.

Deep Canyon offers a challenge to high adventure, as Randall and I learned in 1938 when we joined three friends for a downstream traverse. An ascent would have required the talents of mountaineers having more experience than we had. Normally 'first man over the edge,' I recall an irrelevant event: my pack slipped from my shoulder on the first long rapel, and my Rollieflex was smashed on the rocks below. Years later I realized that the memory of scenes mentally recorded, and the good companionship of the trail, were far more valuable than the immediate utility of a camera. It took us eight hours to travel approximately ten miles. I can testify that the rugged splendor and the variety of desert terrain is reward enough for any physical hardships encountered along the way. Randall tells the story in his own words:

"It was an easy hike down the slope from Pinyon Flats to the floor of the upper gorge, but we carried the necessary tools for more difficult climbing problems which we knew lay ahead. Our equipment included four 100-foot ropes, a sledge hammer, two drill bits, and short lengths of iron pipe which could be used if necessary to be drilled into the rock for belay purposes.

"From our starting point at 3500 feet the sandy channel

provided a good trail at first, but we had not progressed far before the grade became steeper and we had to surmount an increasing number of huge boulders.

"Deep Canyon in July was a chasm containing numberless blue-green pools. Only a small stream of water flowed on the surface, and in many places this disappeared entirely. But underground streams apparently carried a generous supply of water, for we found it necessary to wade, swim, or detour in many places. However, we welcomed occasional dives into pools of cool, clear water, for the temperature in Coachella Valley a few miles away was above the 100-degree mark.

"We found the dominant tree in Deep Canyon to be the native cottonwood. There were about 150 of them along the ten-mile route of our journey. I was disappointed in the small number of palms we found— only 41, including veterans and young trees. Those we saw were growing up on the sidewalls, some 500 or 600 feet above the canyon floor. It is mystifying to see the native palm growing where there is no visible water supply. But the water must be there; otherwise there could be no palms.

"Our first climbing problem was a waterfall with a sheer drop we estimated at 75 feet. But there was an easy detour; we didn't bother to uncoil the ropes. Farther downstream we came to a 12-foot drop where we found it necessary to dive in and swim across a 40-foot pool. We arranged an overhead tramway with the ropes in order to ferry the knapsacks and equipment across the pool.

"No additional difficulties developed until we reached the junction where the Hidden Palms tributary enters the main channel. Around the bend we came suddenly to a 60-foot drop. No detour was possible. Below us lay a pool of blue-green water. We fashioned a suitable belay, and one at a time we lowered ourselves into the pool, where a 30-foot swim was necessary. Again we used a tramway to lower our packs.

"We were now in the most precipitous sector of the gorge, and our progress was sharply downward as we scrambled over boulders and waded or swam through pools that followed one another in close succession.

"Less than a mile from our previous rope-down we came to major waterfall No. 3, a vertical cliff on which grew a thick covering of ferns. Now experienced, we quickly found a belay. I think we felt a trace of disappointment when Mac shouted up that the water was only waist deep.

"We had gone only a short distance when we arrived at another waterfall where a tiny stream dropped over the face. From where we stood we could not see the face of the drop, but we could see the outer edge of the pool. Vertical distances always seem to be magnified when one looks down; we were not sure whether we faced a longer rapel than we had previously encountered.

"It was past midday and we dug into our knapsacks for lunch. While we ate we discussed the possibilities of this descent. To make sure that the first man down would not find himself dangling in midair at the end of his rope we tied two 100-foot ropes together. We took turns with the drill, chiselling out a hole in the granite for a belay pin. Each climber descended in a small stream of water, taking a shower bath as he lowered himself. First man down reported that the 100-foot double strand just reached the surface of the pool. The water was ankle deep; we were missing our swims.

"At the bottom of this waterfall our altimeter showed an elevation of 1650 feet. Below this point we found more pools and a few drops of ten to twelve feet, but only once during the remainder of the trip was it necessary to uncoil the ropes again. A half-mile further the canyon walls began to spread out, and a hot blast of air blew up from the desert floor. We followed the bajada to the 900-foot level, then hiked up the slope to the Palms-to-Pines highway where a driver met us with the car.

"While I have devoted most of this story to the physical problems of traversing the canyon, I want to record my opinion that here, at the back door of the Palm Desert community, is a gorge of such rugged grandeur as to deserve rank as one of the most impressive scenic areas of the desert southwest. And I am sure it will never be crowded with traffic."

This ends Randall's narrative of the Deep Canyon outing. It seems appropriate to add that Randall, in all the years of his desert peak climbing and canyon exploration, never mentioned in his published reports the physical exhaustion, narrow escapes from disaster, and discouragements which sometimes accompanied these expeditions. He enjoyed trips which tested his physical fitness, but he also believed sincerely that each adventure widened his knowledge of the desert he loved and which provided him with new opportunities to introduce others to it.

The seven canyons described in this chapter represent only a very small part of the documentary on palms which Randall published in *Desert* Magazine during nearly twenty years. It would be accurate to say that he was the most active reporter on *Washingtonia's* habitat, and he excited the interest of hundreds of visitors. Less recognized were his excursions into Baja California, where he found palms never before mentioned by white men. Walt Wheelock published in 1971 "Palm Canyons of Baja California" by Randall Henderson (La Siesta Press, Box 406, Glendale, Ca 91209, 72 pp., $1.95) which is a republication of articles appearing in *Desert* Magazine from June 1946 to February 1955. Future botanical historians will record the name of Henderson as the modern discoverer of these beautiful native trees.

It is true that Randall was the chief publicist of the

native palm in his time, but he always cherished a secret joy that many of his favorite canyons would remain inaccessible to men for a very long time. His feeling is expressed in the conclusion of his story about Tajo Canyon below the Mexican border, where he counted 4518 mature trees and described scenes of unrivalled beauty:

"There are too many lovely places on this earth for all of us to see all of them, and perhaps it is just as well for the present that Tajo should enjoy the protection provided by its inaccessibility. The beauty will be there, even if human eyes seldom look upon it. Half the fun of living is dreaming of the places we would like to go, and sensing the fact that Nature is preserving the charm of these hidden beauty spots for the day when perhaps we may have opportunity to see and enjoy them."

8. The Cove Becomes A Community

One of the fastest growing cities of California, Palm Desert is a phenomenon of this generation.

IN THE SUMMER of 1919 my father drove the family Model T from our home in Blythe to Riverside. A carpenter friend sat with him on the front seat; I bounced around on the back seat as Dad struggled all night with the sandy, rutted road across the Chuckawalla Desert. We had breakfast at Mecca and it was still early morning when we passed the sandhills near Indian Wells. I can remember how Dad's friend laughed as he read a crude sign beside the road: FOR SALE. THIS 40 ACRES. SAKRIFISE $60. "What darned fool would spend a dollar and a half an acre on this worthless sand?" He repeated the question a half-dozen times before we got to Palm Springs, interrupting himself to laugh at the foolishness of the idea.

It was twenty-five years later when I walked with Randall Henderson in the area south of Palm Village. Randall had learned that he would have to pay at least $60 *an acre* for unimproved desert land at that time. Another twenty-eight years passed before I began the writing of this book, and I have before me a letter from a man who sold a large parcel of land in Indian Wells for $15,000 an acre, and he added, "My remaining land doubles in price every year." A real estate man told me that a three-acre parcel in Palm Desert sold last year for $100,000.

If land values provide a valid index of "progress" the twenty-five mile cordon between Indio and Palm Springs—with 50,000 vehicles moving daily on paved Highway 111—is a remarkable example of man's adaptability to changing economic conditions. In the two decades after World War II men discovered they needed the open spaces and clean, sunny air of the desert, and they brought their affluence, their aggressiveness, and their avariciousness to the arid lands. Fortunately, they brought their virtues, too. Who can say that "making a buck" in unearned profit is evil when it can be shown that generous support of altruistic movements followed? For the purposes of this record, non-profit enterprises will be emphasized, followed by minimal reference to business organizations.

MEN BUILT, AND BUILT, AND BUILT

Most American cities (or any city, for that matter) normally attribute their origin and growth to man's potential for work: commerce by land and sea, agriculture, manufacture, or extraction of forest-mineral resources. The Deep Canyon cove had none of these potentials; it had only a clean, undisturbed, scenic environment and an exhilarating winter climate.

Within a man's lifetime more than twelve million people had pushed westward to sample coastal southern California's publicized climate, and when they crowded themselves to the point of suffocation those who could afford it sought relief in the desert. Snowbound easterners had accepted the promotion of Palm Springs as the western Garden of Eden, but they found that it, too, had become urbanized; they turned to the fledgling communities to the south and southeast.

U.S. Department of Agriculture studies of the date-growing area of the Valley indicate average January temperatures ranging from 42 to 69 degrees F., July readings range from 72 to 109, and night temperatures for six months of the year below 50 degrees. These figures are confirmed by the annual report of the Palm Desert Chamber of Commerce, although summer residents who remember occasional 120 degree days and sleepless nights tend to forget the annual averages. Rainfall is less than three inches a year, and light snowfall may be seen perhaps once in a decade.

It is fruitless to speculate on the sociological impact of the vanishing work ethic; the point here is that in less than three decades men built a beautiful community in this desert cove, some coming to escape work and others coming to perform useful and profitable services. The alchemy of the desert climate seemed to sponsor creativity and altruism among many, an egoistic concentration on property among others. The cove area that became Palm Desert attracted residents of both persuasions, and they were able to compromise their differences well enough to create a community in which they are taking justifiable pride.

As described in previous chapters, Clifford Henderson founded the Palm Desert Corporation early in 1945 on the recommendation of his older brother, Randall, and with the energetic and able assistance of another brother, Phil. He brought together nineteen wealthy and influential men of the Los Angeles area who advanced $250,000 as initial investment for the promotion and improvement of their 1620-acre townsite in the desert. With land purchasing and engineering studies completed, bulldozers and construction crews went to work in July, 1946. Within a year sixteen miles of surfaced roads and fifteen miles of water lines had been installed, and at the center of the site work had started on the luxurious Shadow Mountain Club. Residential and commercial lots went on the market and a fourth brother, Carl Henderson, was the sales director, succeeded later by Edith Eddy Ward.

Before the star-spangled opening of the Club on December 4, 1948, more than a million dollars worth of homes and commercial buildings had been completed or were under construction. Wide avenues, plantings of palm and other native trees, and generous provision for parking were elements of the early townsite planning. The Palm Desert Corporation was sold in August 1956 to the Baldwin Hills Sales Co. and the Home Savings and Loan Assn., but the sale did not include the Shadow Mountain Club or Firecliff Lodge, the latter retained by Cliff Henderson and Leonard Firestone. Firestone sold his interest in the Lodge the following year. Cliff claimed at this time that $30,000,000 in improvements had been made in the 1800-acre site, including 311 homes, 32 hotels, 53 swimming pools, an expanding shopping area, all utilities, and numerous public buildings.

Construction boomed, not only in the corporation area,

but in all the cove communities. Within two decades unofficial estimates of assessed valuation (one quarter of actual value) were set at $21 million, with a prediction of $43 million by 1980. Some officials of corporate land developments were beginning to talk about a "boom or bust" trend, but investment and construction did not slacken in the early 70s.

Population studies abounded through the 60s. A 1961 study made by the Palm Desert Library board showed 1327 registered voters, a population of 4600, and an assessed valuation of $14 million. A study made by shopping center promoters in 1963 predicted a 1975 population of 39,000, up to 64,000 in 1980. The Los Angeles Bureau of Municipal Research made a 1965 study of a 4.3 square mile area with a population of 7,500, 5,000 dwelling units, and $33 million in valuation. An economic feasibility study by the Coro Corporation in 1966 covered an eight square mile area having 58.82 miles of roadways, a population of 5,830, and an assessed valuation of $22,800,000. The Palm Desert Chamber of Commerce printed population estimates of 8,462 in 1968, upping it to 9,000 the next year. Postal delivery stops, telephone installations, and school enrollments indicated similar trends. The Riverside County Planning Department produced a general plan for development of the cove communities in late 1971, predicting that the area from Indio to Palm Springs would have a population of 81,200 in the year 1980.

Subdivision signs and pennants sprang out of the sand west of Highway 74 and other areas surrounding the original Palm Desert site. A county official last year said Palm Desert was the eleventh fastest growing town in California.

At first building activity concentrated on single family dwelling units, many designed by famous architects, and some were very expensive. Later there was a rush to build condominiums near the new country golf clubs (there were nineteen full-sized courses in western Coachella Valley in

1971, with more being planned); after that a spurt in mobile home parks, followed by construction of hundreds of apartment units. An unofficial record of building permits issued in 1968 added up to $16 million, dropping to $12.3 million in 1970.

Since Cathedral City, Thunderbird, Rancho Mirage, and Palm Desert are unincorporated (hence do not have local building codes), their residents must look to the Riverside County Planning Commission and the County Board of Supervisors for zoning regulations and basic governmental services. Some of the early subdividers controlled standards by rigid deed restrictions or a system of club membership (reportedly including prohibition of sales to non-Caucasians in order to create an "all-rich, all-white" community). Speakers professing a social conscience have protested in vain.

Controversies regarding the number of units per acre, architectural design, and proximity of unwanted development rocked the community for years. The Planning Commission and its staff could always expect delegations of heated citizens from the desert communities. Opposition to Board rulings on the 352-unit, $3.2 million McKeon apartment project west of Highway 74 last year caused the organization of a group named "Concerned Citizens of Palm Desert," and they made demands on the Board to provide for height limits on structures, minimum area and frontage requirements on various types of construction, and curtailment of variance changes during summer months (presumably because many property owners wouldn't be present to air protests).

Palm Desert Country Club Estates, originally a retirement community called Palm City, was bought by a partnership in 1964 and converted into a club membership project. Now having a population approaching 2000, membership in the association includes access to an excellent golf course.

An orderly and attractive commercial area on Palm

Desert Drive paralleling Highway 111 includes shopping centers, offices, restaurants, and specialty shops. Motels, mobile home parks, and other service facilities are conveniently located.

School officials and members of the Chamber of Commerce and men's service clubs talk much about Palm Desert's *growth and progress,* which means continuous increase in population, buying power, and valuations. The phrase suggests that men forget easily, that they will work very hard to create the problems they had only recently sought to escape. The work ethic dies slowly.

PALMS TO PINES HIGHWAY

To cause a broad strip of concrete to be laid south out of Palm Desert to the high vacationland of the San Jacinto Mountains required two decades of effort by Coachella Valley residents. The stories of early pioneers on this road project would fill a book in itself.

In the early years of this century there was a wagon road from Hemet Valley to Vandeventer Flat, but Riverside County did not construct the present highway from the western valley to Idyllwild until 1925-26. About this time J. Win Wilson, editor of the Coachella Valley *Date Palm,* began a vigorous campaign to have the road extended eastward in order to give desert dwellers access to the high country. He became the spokesman for a number of valley organizations in advocacy before the Board of Supervisors and the U.S. Forest Service. The Board requested A.C. Fulmor, county surveyor, to make a preliminary survey; his 1928 report detailed three routes, but he recommended the Pinyon Flats route, which the Board accepted. The county started rebuilding the old wagon road from Mountain Center to Pinyon Flats in 1929.

The County sought federal assistance through Forest Service funds, and in 1930 J.F. Waller, associate highway engineer of the Bureau of Public Roads, made his reconnaissance report. The joint county-federal road project was started in late 1931 and paving was finished in 1933. The Palms-to-Pines Highway, as it was known, was taken into the highway system that year and was redesignated Highway 74 shortly thereafter. The highway from Palm Desert to a point east of Hemet was included in the state's Scenic Highway system last year, permitting prohibition of sign-boards.

Wilson Howell, an Indio date grower, acquired three sections of mountain land in 1927. He had no way of reaching his property except by the circuitous route through Banning and Idyllwild, or by climbing the mountain on foot. He needed a road, and he expended great effort in promoting a construction project. He wanted to improve the place he called Ribbonwood (now Spring Crest); he cut the tough brush and carved out roads by hand. The unique rustic structures he built of native materials attracted passers-by for many years. His dream of building homesites was shattered by advancing age, and he sold out to William Newell in 1965. Newell developed more than a hundred large residential lots and a few sites for hotels, installed a good water system, and built paved roads in the site. But his enthusiasm exceeded his estimate of subdivision costs in that rugged country, and his financial luck ran out within three years. Thirteen families have homes at Spring Crest, but the remaining lots of the subdivision are controlled by a Palm Springs holding company.

Art Nightingale developed a large area at Pinyon Flats about the time the highway was finished, and perhaps a hundred modest cabins have been built near Sugarloaf Mountain. At about the 4000 foot level a development known as Pinyon Crest lies a mile off the highway, and about forty families have built beautiful homes there in the last fifteen years.

In recent years Gwynn Wilson has developed Royal Carrizo nine miles from Palm Desert, consisting of large view sites, carefully landscaped and oriented. The area is well off the highway, guarded by gates, and the dozen or so home-owners have planned with discrimination.

Several years before the highway was built Mr. and Mrs. Steven Shumway, Coachella Valley date growers, home-steaded Section 22 near Asbestos Mountain and north of Pinyon Flats. Mrs. Nina Paul Shumway, now a resident of Tucson, is author of a book, "Your Desert and Mine," which describes the problems and difficulties they encountered in their pioneering venture, and becomes lyrical in describing the massive views of desert terrain from the 4300 foot level. They built a beautiful home there, "The Tors," largely using local stone. The property is now owned and occupied by Frances Rich, noted sculptress; her mother, Irene Rich, cele-brated movie actress of the 30s, has a home nearby.

Tony Burke, Palm Springs real estate broker for more than forty years, has a home at Spring Crest, and he prefers to commute to his office. He has become almost poetic in describing the beauty of his home environment: "I can't think of moving back to the low desert."

Burke's enthusiasm is shared by scores of Coachella Val-ley residents who own homes on the mountain, or who find relief from summer heat by retreating to the high country for vacations. It was made possible by a small group of desert people who dreamed and fought more than forty years ago for a road down the mountainside.

JACKRABBIT HOMESTEADERS

President Franklin D. Roosevelt on June 1, 1938, signed into law the Small Tract Act, which authorized the Secretary of the Interior to dispose of certain public lands. Two years later Secretary Ickes detailed the terms and conditions under which five-acre tracts could be leased, and providing for issuance of deeds after specified improvements had been completed. Not until late 1944 were applications accepted by the U.S. Land Office in Los Angeles. By February, 1945, Registrar Paul B. Witmer reported that he had 1500 applications on hand for sections in southern California, including Section 36 in the hill area at the southwest edge of the Deep Canyon cove. By the end of 1945 the entire 128 parcels of the 640-acre section in the cove had been taken up.

Land Office surveyors had not established corner posts for the five-acre plots; only a chart indicating the lot number was available for locating the sites. Randall and I and three of his associates on *Desert* Magazine staff were among the earliest applicants, and we lost no time in trying to find our "homestead." His editorial page of March, 1945, partially described our problem:

"The formula for locating one of these jackrabbit homesites is to comb the desert over until you find a government section corner within a reasonable distance, say a mile or so, of the spot where you think your five acres are located. Then look at your watch and take a slant at the sun, and decide which way is north or east, or whatever direction you want to go. Then start pacing off the distance, three feet to a step. If you have made a perfect guess as to compass direction, and if every pace is exactly three feet long, eventually you will arrive at your desert homesite.

"But there may be two or three mini-mountain ranges along the route, so you have to allow for the short steps going up hill and the skidding going down. And when you come face to face with a boulder as big as a house you have to do a bit of "offset surveying" to get around it."

The problem of precise location was so confusing that Section 36 leasees in 1947 contributed to a fund to employ a

Riverside civil engineer to establish corners for each parcel. Once corners were set, homesteaders could proceed with improvements necessary in order to apply for deeds. I surrendered my lease many years ago, but I walked the section this year out of curiosity, and I like to think that my dream-plot was where an attractive stone house now rests atop a craggy hill.

In 1953 many attractive homes had been built in the section, and Mrs. Arnold Schaak and Robert Waters organized the Cahuilla Hills Improvement Association, an active civic group. With united action the group obtained road-grading service from the county, and within three years they had electric power service from the California Power Company. By 1959 telephone service was available throughout the area. Forming a water district in 1966, the association promoted the passage of a $1,200,000 bond issue and entered a contract with the Coachella Valley County Water District to provide a pressure water system.

The Cahuilla Hills area has not been included in the various incorporation moves by Palm Desert, although it is considered to be a respected segment of the Palm Desert community. Home-owners there have obtained the public services and utilities they consider adequate, and their association serves them well on a range of common interests. Mrs. Mora Brown, a former member of the *Desert* Magazine staff, is currently the president of the Cahuilla Hills Improvement Association.

PALM VILLAGE

About the time the Palms-to-Pines Highway was built, William A. Johnson owned 440 acres north of the Indio-Palm Springs road which he had acquired from King C. Gillette. The land was planted to grapefruit, interplanted with date palms. Johnson was founder of American Pipe and Construction Company, and Gillette's name was associated with the earliest safety razors and shaving blades.

In 1935 Johnson began the subdivision of approximately fifty residential lots, and three years later the Mollin Investment Company acquired an interest and assumed the management of the holdings. When Johnson participated in the construction of Shasta Dam in 1942, he sold his interest to the Mollin organization, which promoted the subdivision they named Palm Village. (Randall Henderson's initial contact with Mollin executives is described in Chapter 5.)

Christopher Hendra, president of Mollin (with offices now located in Arcadia), wrote Randall: "We had very little activity during the war, but late in 1944 sales picked up and by 1948 we had subdivided the entire 440 acres. In addition we purchased from King Gillette Jr. the sixty acres facing south along Highway 111 and subdivided that. In 1948 we sold our remaining interest to I.C. Stearns of Palm Springs, who was prepared to finance home construction."

In 1953 the 180 home-owners in the Village formed a community services district in order to acquire the privately-owned water company then serving the community. Harry O. Davis and Werner Gubitz secured an option to purchase and residents voted 98 to 4 in favor of forming the services district. Subsequently a $150,000 bond issue was approved to purchase the water company and to enter other community services. Gubitz was named secretary and general manager, a position he held competently for many years. There are now more than 850 meters in the community water system, and the district is seeking to extend its services by creating a public park.

Since the establishment of the Palm Desert post office in 1947, Palm Village has been considered a part of the Palm Desert community, and the area has been included in four incorporation movements. ⋞§ 116 §⋟

GENERAL PATTON'S MOTOR POOL

Troops of General George S. "Old Blood and Guts" Patton's Third Army used Camp Young (several hundred square miles of the Chuckawalla and Mojave Deserts) for training in armoured warfare. During the months of rugged training the outfit needed an intermediate location, and officers literally confiscated a large area of the Palm Desert cove for use as a practice sector in deployment under air attack, and later as an installation for repair of motor vehicles.

Owners of the land testify they were neither consulted nor compensated in the matter, and the U.S. Adjutant General's office has not responded to requests for historical details (it may be assumed that some acts in the national defense will remain honorable if quietly ignored). Pioneer residents of the area remember, however, that there was great activity in the cove during 1943-44, with caravans of trucks and carriers coming and going.

Third Army technicians removed the cove installations early in 1944, the same year the invincible armoured battalions swept across France to force an early termination of the war in Europe. General Patton, the flamboyant pistol-packing Californian, died in France in 1945, and the war ended. The last vestiges of army activity in the cove were large blocks of foundation concrete which were removed when developers of Shadow Mountain Club began landscaping operations.

INDIAN WELLS

The late E.M. Peterson, a former property management executive and member of the San Marino city council, came to the area east of Palm Desert in 1956 to found a community development. He bought Rancho Palmeras from Jack McKenzie, followed by acquisition of groves and vineyards from Kenneth Lichty, Bert Ripple, and Robert Webb.

His residential development moved rapidly, and the new owners organized in 1957 to form the Indian Wells Area Property Owners Association, later adding "Eldorado" to the title. Eldorado Country Club Estates was one of the early developments, and its fabulous golf course attracted VIPs from all over the country, accounting in large part for the later fame of the townsite. The group employed a planning department. The association agreed to create a high class residential, country club, and resort hotel community, and their proposed zoning restrictions were officially approved.

The association in 1966 moved that "in order to control our local taxes and control the planning of orderly growth" it should create its own local government. It immediately filed official notice of intent to incorporate. The incorporation election in 1967 (88 per cent of registered voters casting) revealed that 93 per cent favored forming a city government (said to be the highest percentage ever recorded in California history), and on July 14, 1967, Indian Wells became the 400th incorporated city in California.

Peterson, a member of the board of directors of the property owners association and its president for three years, was elected to the first city council. He was named mayor, a position he filled until his death in November, 1971. He said early last year that there were approximately 760 homes in the city, housing 1500 people, "but because some of these are second homes our official population was set back to 890." Official Riverside County records for 1968 showed a population of 933, with assessed valuation of $13,700,070 and a per capita valuation of $14,684. Unofficial estimates since then suggest a per capita figure as high as $22,000, and reporters have written that most homes can be valued at $100,000 to $1,000,000.

Mayor "Pete" was proud of the wealth of his community,

its prohibition of objectionable commercial establishments and signs, and its low (five to fifteen cents per $100 of valuation) tax to operate the city government. He said a civic center site had been purchased and a city hall will be built without a bond issue. "It has not been the intention of the city to grow large," he said, "but rather to develop a small, desirable, planned and protected low-density residential community, retaining our beautiful desert oasis character."

Early fame came to Indian Wells when President Dwight D. Eisenhower spent several winters at the Eldorado Country Club, a beautifully landscaped garden spot lying at the center of the city. Royalty also touched base here when Prince Philip of England, husband of Queen Elizabeth, played polo at the Eldorado Polo Club. Television coverage of the great and near-great on the greens during the winter season brought national and world-wide publicity to the desert community.

Harry Truman visited his friend, former Governor Mon Wallgren of Washington, who maintained a home in Palm Desert for several years. John F. Kennedy came to Palm Desert three times, staying at the home owned by Bing Crosby. Lyndon Johnson came to the desert several times to confer briefly with Gen. Eisenhower. President Nixon has visited several times, usually staying at the estate of Ambassador to England Walter Annenberg.

In terms of man's capacity to mold his environment, Indian Wells has indeed come a long way from the time when a band of half-clad Indians squatted beside their dug well at the base of a barren sandhill.

PALM DESERT INCORPORATION

Four times in the last nine years citizens of this community have tried to make Palm Desert a legally-designated city— and each attempt has failed. Although the will to continue the fight for cityhood remains alive, postmortem studies suggest that the failures of 1963-70 had many bases.

The community was very young—less than twenty years old—and it sprang from diverse cultures without a central unifying agency. The residents naturally joined voluntary associations— 34 were identified in 1968— and each interpreted its relationship to the total community in different ways. Although various groups had suggested the creation of a "Cove Communities Coordinating Council," such a body did not exist for the purposes of incorporation sponsors. Although extensive and detailed studies were made by professional investigators prior to each of the incorporation efforts, there was apparently a wide misunderstanding among residents regarding the functions and responsibilities that could or should be accepted by the proposed city and the probable cost in relation to subventions from county and state and receipts from non-tax sources.

Suggested here are only a few of the reasons why Palm Desert is not yet a city; no doubt there are others. There is good reason to believe that the community will eventually achieve local government, but only after all associations and non-committed citizens unite in common purpose. This will require leadership and dedication of a high order; in final analysis that is what the community has lacked during the last decade.

Briefly, a review of abortive efforts in the past may be enlightening. In April, 1963, a Palm Desert Cityhood Committee circulated petitions for an incorporation election and got strong opposition from a group identified as Desert Community Association. Petitions were inadequate and the movement died.

In October, 1966, another group began with months of careful study, and proposed incorporation of an area of approximately twenty-six sections. Residents of the Indian

Wells-Eldorado Country Club area to the east had stated their reasons for not wanting to be included in the proposed area, and they launched a speedy and successful campaign to create their own municipality. This action reduced the area and assessed valuation of the proposed townsite plat; petitions turned in to the county clerk did not contain the names of twenty-five per cent of the owners of assessed property in the area, and they were declared invalid.

A third effort got under way in September, 1968, when the county's Local Agency Formation Commission directed the county administrative officer to make a feasibility study of thirty-eight sections between Palm Springs and Indio. The study, which included the communities of Cathedral City, Thunderbird Ranch, Palm Desert, Palm Desert Country Club Estates, and La Quinta, revealed an assessed valuation of $59 million, a population of 22,869 with 7,623 registered voters, and 149.4 miles of county roads.

A public meeting in January, 1969, attended by about four hundred residents of the areas involved, made it clear that the study areas involved were too large for their definition of "home rule," and the plan was unacceptable. Thus, for the third time, an incorporation movement died before it could be submitted to a vote of the public involved.

Early in 1970 a citizens committee with Duane Wheeler as chairman began a long study which was published during the spring, suggesting a much smaller area for possible incorporation. County officials provided authentic and current information to document the study, and city managers throughout California provided data for comparison. Probable city revenues from taxes, licenses, fees, and permits were spelled out, as well as possible city subventions from collections by the county and state. The detailed financial study suggested the necessity of a city tax of seventy-four cents per $100 valuation. The committee proposed that the cost was low in comparison with Indio's $1.13 and Palm Spring's $2.13. They postulated that the owner of a small home would have a city tax of $33 a year, and a large home as high as $95 a year. The area of the study covered only the towns of Palm Desert and Rancho Mirage. For the first time petitions were valid and acceptable, and voters went to their polls on December 1, 1970.

But the careful study failed to convince. The vote was 1049 for incorporation, 1435 against. Seventy-three per cent of eligible voters registered their opinions. Only two of the nine precincts in the two communities favored incorporation; Rancho Mirage voted almost 4 to 1 against it.

One observer said that when the growing pains of adolescence wear off, mature judgment may logically follow. That may be a prejudiced observation, but it indicates a probability that the fifth incorporation movement will be under way before this book gets in print.

COLLEGE OF THE DESERT

Ten-year-old College of the Desert, occupying an eight million dollar plant on a 160-acre site at the north edge of Palm Desert, enrolls 2000 full-time and part-time day students. Dr. Roy C. McCall is its president, a position he has held as its administrative head since the origin of the two-year community college.

Located in mid-valley, it is the only higher education institution in the western desert area and it serves students from all parts of Coachella Valley. Gifted with an excellent faculty having a high percentage of advanced academic degrees, COD has established an enviable scholastic record, and has provided a center for major cultural activities of the valley.

About the time the first buildings were being erected in

Palm Desert, the boards of trustees of the Coachella Valley Union High School District and the Palm Springs Unified School District jointly discussed the possibility of creating a higher education institution for the valley, and they sought the aid of executives from the State Department of Education.

Surveys of student need and financial feasibility were not completed until 1957. The report from Sacramento projected that within five years high school enrollments and the tax base from assessed valuation would be more than sufficient to justify the creation of a college district. With that assurance, the two boards obtained authorization to hold an election. On January 21, 1958, voters approved the formation of a community college district by a ratio of nearly 10 to 1.

The five members of the first board of trustees elected on April 15 were Donald H. Mitchell, Ray Rummonds, David M. McGahey, Francis A. Purcell, and William A. Mason. Three were residents of Palm Springs, one from Coachella, and one from Indio. First tasks of the new board were to employ administrators and select and purchase a suitable site. They invited D. Gail Brumwell, who had been an active advocate of the college, to serve as business manager, and he agreed to take a leave of absence from the superintendency of the Coachella Valley High School, a position he had held for fifteen years.

The board made important decisions in 1959. In April it announced appointment of John Carl Warnecke of San Francisco, renowned architect, to supervise the design of the proposed plant, and four Palm Springs architectural firms were named to handle structural details. Brumwell laid before the board twenty-three offers of land available, which they narrowed down to four locations in the Rancho Mirage-Palm Desert-Indian Wells area. They finally selected the 160-acre Odell Ranch.

In July Dr. McCall accepted an offer of the presidency

of the college. He had earned his master's and doctoral degrees at the University of Iowa; had taught speech, drama, and English at College of the Pacific and the University of Oregon; and had served for five years as president of Modesto Junior College. When asked why he had left a secure position at an established institution to pioneer a new school in the desert, he replied, "I was impressed with the calibre of the trustees of the new district. The financial strength of the desert community offered potential for a fine development. The dream of developing a new institution was intriguing. And in addition, the desert had a special attraction for Velma and me."

Before the end of the year—October 14—voters of the district approved a $3,500,000 bond issue by a vote of 3476 to 1724, in excess of the required two-thirds majority. This funded the land purchase and provided for the first stage of construction. To provide for additional classrooms, a gymnasium, and a library, voters passed two more issues: $2,000,-000 in 1964 and $2,500,000 in 1968.

The new buildings were opened in September, 1962, for an initial enrollment of 525 full time day students; by the 1971 fall semester that enrollment had almost quadrupled. Due to a disproportionately high adult population in the district, 1971-72 enrollment in extended day (night) classes approximately doubled the number of day students. It is also evident that adults wish to use continuing education and cultural opportunities offered.

The master plan for the college proposed construction of a Cultural Arts Center to cost approximately six million dollars. It envisioned a performing arts building with a theater to seat 2000 or more, a visual arts building to house a gallery and art school, and a music hall for recitals and instrumental instruction. Planners originally assumed that financing such a center must necessarily be postponed into the distant future, but rapidly increasing enrollments and corresponding demands on college facilities—especially in the performing arts—have caused friends of the college to urge earlier construction of the cultural complex.

A bequest of the late Pearl McCallum of $250,000 and other substantial private gifts have suggested that the Center could be funded by 1975 without waiting for availability of tax resources. An illustrated brochure has been published, inviting gifts and pledges, and optimism has been expressed that the Center could be built without a bond issue.

At present the college gymnasium serves as a makeshift auditorium, and it has drawn capacity attendance for numerous dramatic and musical events throughout the school year. Proximity of talented artists and entertainers and acceptance of the college by the community suggest that construction of an adequate arts unit should not be postponed.

Dr. McCall, who confessed this year that he looked forward to retirement soon, expressed the hope that he might see the new center realized in his present contract term. "We could do some magnificent things if we had the kind of facility we are planning. There is no doubt in my mind that we we will be able to fund it, but how long it will take is another matter." He went on to comment that the college is sure to grow, with a potential of a thousand added students from the high desert country to the north. BLM land near Coachella is available, he said, for a small college annex "to be near the people."

Growth of college enrollment has made possible the expansion of academic programs (in addition to the basic subjects, humanities, and social and natural sciences) to include vocational courses in nursing, horticulture, technology, and business education. More science units are needed, and the music curriculum needs to be refined, the president added.

In 1967 the Morongo Unified School District was annexed to the original Coachella Valley Community College District, adding 1358 square miles to the original 4000 square mile district. The added area has an assessed valuation of $63 million and a population of 20,000.

Two of the original members of the board of trustees remain in their responsible positions after fourteen years: Mr. Mitchell and Mr. Rummonds. They are now joined by Helen K. Staley and Robert Taylor of Palm Springs and John Outcault of Palm Desert. There were only thirty-five instructors on the faculty when the college opened; that number had increased to 110 full-time teachers during the 1971-72 year, plus many more part-time instructors.

DEEP CANYON DESERT RESEARCH CENTER

The great chasm on the north slope of the Santa Rosa Mountains which through the ages disgorged most of the sand and rock on which Palm Desert is now built is known as Deep Canyon (described on pages 100-103).

Philip L. Boyd in 1959 gave 3600 acres of land at the mouth of Deep Canyon to the University of California to be added to its land and water reserves system. An additional 6400 acres of public land adjoining the Boyd tract was set aside by the U.S. Bureau of Land Management for research purposes, and the total area of about 10,000 acres was named the Philip L. Boyd Deep Canyon Research Center.

Boyd in 1940 had bought 273 acres about a half-mile south of Highway 111, and he and his family and guests used the butte at the center of the site for picnics and barbeques. Then mayor of Palm Springs, rancher, and land developer, after the war he became a state assemblyman representing Riverside County. He built ranch houses on the property and enjoyed horseback riding into the canyon about four miles south. He admired the beauty of the terrain and he obtained several sections which he later turned over to the University after the governor appointed him a member of U.C. Board of Regents. He stipulated two provisions: that the area should be preserved in its wild state, and that research should be encouraged and promoted in desert ecology.

The research center was established at the mouth of the Deep Canyon gorge in 1962 with buildings designed to provide living and working quarters for as many as four researchers at one time. A radio-telephone permits outside communication, but electric power did not become available until 1969. A paved lane provides the only access to the laboratory, and a locked gate and steel fence have been built across the floodplain to prevent unauthorized entry.

More than fifteen sections of the reserve range in altitude from 700 to 4600 feet, and the terrain consists of precipitous canyon walls, sandy washes, and an extensive alluvial fan. It contains abundant mammalian wild life—more than forty species have been identified so far—as well as scores of species of insect and reptilian life. Botanists, too, find the area a fruitful place for study of plant adaptation to arid conditions. Some important and original studies have been published since the Reserve was established.

Desert bighorn sheep (*Ovis canadensis*) live at the higher elevations, and an estimated 350 individuals remain. Mule deer are frequently seen on the higher slopes.

Resident naturalist of the Research Center is Lloyd Tevis, Jr. of Rancho Mirage. He was host to University President Charles Hitch and other distinguished guests at the dedication March 7, 1970, when a bronze plaque was placed in recognition of Regent Boyd's gift to the public.

LIVING DESERT RESERVE

At Palm Desert's back door is a two-compartment class-room designed for the study of plant and animal life of the lower Sonoran life zone. One is the Philip L. Boyd Desert Research Center described above; the other is the Living Desert Reserve, a 360-acre portion of the Deep Canyon bajada lying north of the University's fenced area.

The Research Center is reserved for scholarly study by advanced students of ecological balance; the Living Reserve is open to lay people who want to stroll nature trails in order to learn something about the common denizens of the desert.

Since the middle 1940s the Coachella Valley County Water District has owned the sections in which the Deep Canyon bajada drains northeastward toward the Whitewater channel, and has built dikes and check dams in order to control the seasonal runoffs which have threatened the new developments to the north. Because the area has been despoiled by careless campers and plant robbers, Phil Boyd and Randall Henderson initiated a plan to set aside a portion as a desert sanctuary. Boyd, one of the original trustees of the Palm Springs Desert Museum, arranged a 50-year lease with the District for use of the area now known as the Living Desert Reserve. Henderson helped lay out the first paths in the area in 1953, and solicited the interest of scientists and conservation-minded friends.

Early in 1970 the Desert Museum created a separate division known as the Living Desert Association, with its own board of governors. Within the year more than two hundred contributing members had been enrolled in the association, and they approved a proposal to erect an exhibit-headquarters building and employ a naturalist-in-charge. In May the association employed Miss Karen Sausman, a Palm Springs science teacher (now Mrs. George Fowler), as resident naturalist, and with the aid of volunteer labor, she began preparation of permanent trails and exhibit gardens.

Boyd, chairman of the Deep Canyon committee, announced, in July, 1971, that a $50,000 grant from the McCallum Desert Foundation and contributions of $40,000 from association members had made it possible to secure building permits for two buildings. John Outcault, Palm Desert architect, contributed the plans, and designed two stone-surfaced structures that fit beautifully in the environment. Facilities in McCallum Hall, dedicated January 29, 1972, include an exhibit area, meeting room for lectures and nature programs; another building contains headquarters offices and living quarters for the caretaker. Grading for car access and parking was also completed.

Trails in the Reserve are flanked by exhibit shelters and plant specimens are identified by markers and plaques. When all educational units have been installed, it will be possible for a visitor to gain an understanding of the natural desert as an inter-related whole.

First officers of the association's board of governors included Lucien W. Shaw, president; Lloyd Tevis, Jr., vice president; Harrison S. Dimmitt, secretary; and Roy F. Hudson, treasurer. Philip Boyd is the current president. The dedication marked the 85th birthday of Advisor Edmund Jaeger.

The Reserve is open to the public daily, 9 to 5 except Monday, and can be reached by driving to the southern end of Portola Avenue out of Palm Desert.

PALM DESERT PUBLIC LIBRARY

For more than forty years Riverside County supervisors had contracted with the Riverside city library to supply books and limited service to those unincorporated communities that wanted branch libraries. In the early 1950s pioneer residents of the new Palm Desert community began to discuss the idea of establishing a library under the county system.

The late Dr. Edward C. Ruge and Dr. Martin P. Baker visited the Riverside city librarian and received assurance of cooperation if the community would provide suitable housing and necessary library equipment. Cyria A. Henderson, newly-installed president of the Palm Desert Woman's Club, obtained pledges in 1954 from six local organizations to underwrite a $600 a year rental on a room at the Larkspur Lane Patio, owned by Mr. and Mrs. Robert Hanson.

A local library committee was formed with Dr. Ruge as chairman, with representatives from five organizations in the community. The committee had its first meeting January 20, 1955, and Clarice Cavanagh was elected secretary. The first librarian was Nancy Ann Whitehouse, succeeded later in the year by Mrs. Janet James. In the spring of 1956, when monthly book circulation reached 645, the library committee discussed the possibility of erecting a community hall which would contain quarters for the library. A site for this purpose was offered by Mr. and Mrs. Randall Henderson at the intersection of Portola Avenue and Shadow Mountain Drive.

In April, 1958, the committee selected Architect John Outcault to prepare plans for the proposed structure. The Woman's Club announced an initial contribution of $3500 to the project. Two months later the Palm Desert Community Library Association was incorporated, with Phil Franklin as president. In January, 1962, Hal Kapp, Palm Desert realtor, replaced Franklin and has retained the position in the years since.

Carl Henderson accepted chairmanship of the building committee, and he obtained pledges from eleven residents to secure a loan of $39,000 from the Bank of America. Backers were Mrs. Marge Brown, Harry Cannon, Carl Henderson, Clifford Henderson, Carl Jensen, Hal Kapp, Richard C. Kite,

John L. Moon, John Outcault, Ted Smith, and Ed Welcome. None of the pledgees have ever been required to pay on their commitments. Carl was able to report at the end of the next year that many additional donations had been received, the initial loan was about half paid off, and the value of the new building and its grounds was in excess of $75,000, without a penny of taxation. Randall's gift of the three-acre site was valued at $30,000. During the planning period it was decided to abandon the original concept of a community hall; the library stands alone on its landscaped site at the center of the town.

Bernice Lofland was librarian for several years, retiring in 1970. She was succeeded by Mrs. George (Pat) Service, who reported that the 1971 circulation of books had reached 54,000. Jane Kuehner is assistant librarian. An excellent children's library has been provided, and juvenile story programs are attracting the younger set.

Ground-breaking was held at the site May 11, 1962, and dedication of the completed building was March 23, 1963. A bronze plaque in the lobby bears the names of principal contributors to the library building fund, headed by the name Randall Henderson, land donor and one of the library's most ardent supporters.

Randall had demonstrated his belief in the power of the printed word.

EISENHOWER MEDICAL CENTER

On November 27, 1971, the five-million dollar 140-bed Eisenhower Hospital, first of three great buildings to comprise the $7,500,000 Eisenhower Medical Center on Bob Hope Drive in north Palm Desert, was dedicated before a crowd of 17,000. President Richard Nixon, Vice President Spiro Agnew, and Governor Ronald Reagan were principal speakers. The dedication was in memory of President Ike, who was a frequent winter visitor to Palm Desert before his death in 1969.

General Eisenhower, then President, visited the Eldorado Country Club in 1959, and returned with his wife each winter until 1968. Comedian Bob Hope, wise-cracking friend of Presidents and four-star generals, and world-travelling cheerer of U.S. troops, frequently played golf with the President. "Ike's" friendship for Hope, combined with his love of golf, caused Hope to conceive the idea of a desert memorial to the President, and in 1966 he donated an 80-acre tract (valued at $500,000) in Palm Desert to be used for a community hospital.

Hope had only begun his charity at that point: he was star and master of ceremonies at a $1000-a-plate banquet in New York in January, 1970, raising more than a million and a half dollars. He did the same in Los Angeles in April, 1971, and the added contribution to the Center's growing fund was $1,865,000.

As chairman and star performer of the annual Bob Hope Desert Classic, a golf spectacular since the early 1960s, he helped to raise from $100,000 to $350,000 a year for desert-based charities, including seventy per cent of profits directed to the Eisenhower Medical Center. The Classic has become a winter "must" for the rich and powerful; social events during the week take over the calendar in the cove communities. The 1972 Classic, held February 9-13, featured 140 professional golfers, as well as many motion picture stars and TV and sports celebrities. Courses used this year were La Quinta, Eldorado, Bermuda, and Indian Wells.

Fund-raising dinners and other star-studded events in the cove communities during the last three winters made it possible for the EMC board of directors to announce that the first unit of the great medical center was fully funded before the dedication, and without taxation (except for those who chose to donate).

Mrs. Dolores Hope, Bob's wife and a singing star in her own right, is president of EMC. In the spring of 1969 she was formally installed (at a Center Fund dinner) as "honorary mayor" of Palm Desert, a position she still holds. Her comedian husband, who has been "honorary mayor" of Palm Springs for two decades, commented: "It's strange to have another honorary mayor in the family, which goes to prove that politics don't make strange bedfellows."

BOB HOPE DESERT CLASSIC

The winter golf spectacular referred to above began with the Thunderbird Open in 1952, which was discontinued in 1959. In 1960 a new format called the Palm Springs Desert Golf Classic introduced the idea of a five-day, 90-hole tournament for amateurs and professionals playing on four golf courses. For the first time the Classic donated a modest $15,050 to desert charities.

In 1965 Bob Hope accepted the presidency of the Classic; the charity donation that year of $169,150 included a $50,000 personal donation from Hope. In the first twelve years of the Classic $2,091,858 has been turned over to thirty-five desert-based charities in Coachella Valley, including $1,309,528 for the Eisenhower Medical Center. Each year the amount available for charity has increased; in 1971 it was $399,950.

America's leading golfers consider the Classic a "must," partly because of exposure to nation-wide television and partly because the winner's purse is the richest in the PGA tour. Top scorers this year took $145,000; the winner got $29,000. Golfers who have won the Classic in recent years—often in "sudden death" finishes—include Arnold Palmer, Billy Maxwell, Jack Nicklaus, Tommy Jacobs, Doug Sanders, and Billy Casper.

SCHOOLS

The first public school to serve the area was organized in 1916 with ten pupils and one teacher, and was located near Point Happy. The rural district later merged with the Indio School District. H. L. "Bert" Cavanagh, present mayor of Indian Wells, was for many years a trustee of the original school district.

Students from Palm Desert originally attended the Coachella Valley Union High School west of Thermal, riding in an open bus once driven by W.W. "Bill" Cook. Cook, a pioneer date grower, was later to become a Riverside County Supervisor, representing the Fourth District. High school students have been attending Indio High School since the origin of Palm Desert, although an estimated enrollment of 500 is now evident in the area. The need for a high school locally is being currently canvassed.

The first educational institution in Palm Desert was the George Washington elementary school, built on a six-acre site at the intersection of Portola Avenue and Chicory Street in 1949. With an initial enrollment of 200 pupils, the plant provides for a capacity of 394, but peak enrollments have reached 560 for kindergarten through eighth grade; additional classrooms were built in 1961 to serve the increasing enrollment. Principal Patrick K. Kearney has a staff of fourteen teachers. Dr. Harold Schoenfeld is superintendent of the eight school Desert Sands Elementary School District.

The Abraham Lincoln School at 74-100 Rutledge was built in 1965 on a twenty-acre site with an initial enrollment of 160 for grades kindergarten through five. On the same site is the Middle School for grades six, seven, and eight, serving the upper levels that formerly used Washington School. Elementary grades last year enrolled 381 students with thirteen teachers; the Middle School had 336 students with seventeen teachers. Everett F. Johnson is the principal.

The pressure of increasing enrollments in these schools has stimulated studies of creating a new school to be located in the La Quinta-Bermuda area.

CHURCHES

There are eight churches in the Palm Desert area, demonstrating the high level of Christian devotion and altruism that motivated the creation of these lovely places of worship.

The first was a protestant community church. Using a three-acre site on Portola Avenue contributed by the Palm Desert Corporation in 1947, a small group of pioneer residents raised funds for the construction of a small church. They invited the dynamic and colorful Dr. John Robertson McCartney to be the pastor of their Palm Desert Community Church, a position he accepted and held until his retirement in 1952. The group worshiped out of doors or at member homes during construction. It is true that many who attended services arrived on horseback, and a long hitching post was the initial installation at the site. Cliff Henderson was instrumental in providing the land; his brother Carl was chairman of the building committee.

Among the first public buildings in town, the church provided meeting places for the Christian Science Society, the Catholic Sisters, and other early groups. During the pioneer years Dr. McCartney frequently said, "What we need is Grace, Gumption, and Greenbacks. God will provide the Grace, I've got the Gumption, and the people will provide the Greenbacks." His prediction was accurate: the three G's were clearly evident as the church grew in membership and property.

Dr. Dean Miller assumed the pastorate in 1961, coming from the Westminster Presbyterian Church in Oxnard. In

December of that year President Dwight Eisenhower worshipped at the church and he and Mamie continued to return each winter until 1968.

In 1966 the church property on Portola Avenue was sold to a nonprofit corporation to be modified into a community youth center. A larger sanctuary and Christian Education building was built on Highway 74, and the former President, who had taken a personal interest in the new construction, spoke at dedications in February and April. When President Eisenhower died in March 1969 Dr. Miller flew to Abilene, Kansas, to participate in the funeral services.

The present magnificent church, said to be one of the most beautiful sanctuaries in southern California, contains an Eisenhower memorial room and pews purchased by the President.

First religious services of the Sacred Heart Church were held in the unfinished lounge of the Shadow Mountain Club in April, 1948, with Father Joseph Leissler of the Cathedral City church in charge. While a church edifice was under construction at Avenue 44 and Deep Canyon Road in the early 1950s, services were held in a store building on Highway 111. The new church building was ready in 1958, made possible through the tireless efforts of Father A. G. Edwards and the generosity of his congregation. The next year, under the guidance of Father John Desmond, the church considered the creation of youth recreation facilities, but the Youth Center on adjoining land was not completed until 1969, rendering an important additional service to the community. Father Leonard Scannell is the priest this year.

Hope Lutheran Church held its first meetings at the Fairway Cafe in August, 1960, with the Rev. E. Davis Natwick as the pastor. It occupied its own church building at 45-900 Portola Avenue on February 18, 1961. The Rev. Daryl Bjerke came to the church in July, 1968, and he organized a steering committee for the purpose of establishing a young people's facility which ultimately resulted in the dedication of the Christina Sinatra Teen Center on Portola Avenue.

After informal meetings at the home of Carl Henderson, residents of the community who had held membership elsewhere in the Christian Science Church met in August, 1955, (and for five years thereafter) at the *Desert* Magazine building. Late the next year the first lectures were given by Forrest White and Lyle Nixon selected as readers. First regular meetings in the new $130,000 church building at Portola Avenue and Larrea Street were held in January, 1960. The society received recognition as a branch of the mother church February 9, 1961. A reading room, open daily, is maintained at 73-907 Highway 111.

St. Margaret's Episcopal Church of Palm Desert began in 1963 as a mission created by the warden and rector of the Palm Springs church. With the donation of three acres of land on Highway 74 by Mr. and Mrs. Leonard Firestone and Mr. and Mrs. W. A. Moncrief, a building campaign was launched, and the parish hall was dedicated on August 15, 1965. The Rev. Peter J. Brownlee was the first priest. A manse for the priest was built later; within three years of its founding the church property had been fully financed by the congregation without seeking aid from the bishop.

Other churches in the area on which historical data was not made available include the First Baptist Church on Santa Rosa Way, the United Church of Palm City, and St. John's American Lutheran Church.

MEN'S SERVICE CLUBS

The Palm Desert Rotary Club held its charter night program at the Shadow Mountain Club December 15, 1948, with Clifford W. Henderson as its first president. Rotary is an international service club having 707,500 members in 149 countries; the 15,025 local clubs admit only one member from each line of business. The local club has initiated many projects for community betterment, and it provides a useful forum for discussion of business and professional problems. For years the club met at the Shadow Mountain Club.

The Palm Desert Lions Club, with an initial membership of twenty-two, was founded in 1963 under sponsorship of Cathedral City Lions and Delmont Ziegler and Wayne Kizer as local organizers. It holds dinner meetings twice a month at the Whispering Waters dining room in Rancho Mirage. One of its local projects is decorating the business district with American flags on national holidays. Its sight preservation program includes providing equipment for testing children's eyes at local elementary schools.

The "Friend of the Boy" organization in Palm Desert is the local chapter of International Optimist Clubs, chartered in 1959 with an initial membership of thirty-seven business and professional men. Ben F. Arnold was the first president. Interested in the promotion of civic affairs, the club's special project is the encouragement of good citizenship among boys.

OTHER CIVIC ORGANIZATIONS

After a long career on the vaudeville circuit, Clay Stearns came to Coachella Valley in June, 1948, to become a real estate salesman as an associate of his brother, I. C. Stearns, who had purchased the Mollin interests in Palm Village. Clay's interests caused him to form a Little Theatre group, and in 1951 he staged a premier performance before a packed audience in a small improvised playhouse. In the years following Clay and his associates enlisted professional and amateur talent to stage periodic theatrical productions, most popular of which was the annual Palm Desert Follies. With financial assistance from the community, the group purchased a site and erected a Little Theatre building to serve the community. But, unfortunately, Clay moved on to other stages, and the Players disbanded a few years later.

Twenty-seven women responded in 1949 to an invitation from Mrs. Floyd Mitchell to meet at her home for the purpose of forming an auxiliary for the fledgling community church. They named Mrs. Minnie Burdon as president and chose the name of Desert Guild. In October, 1954, the Guild's roster had grown and the membership interests had broadened; it reorganized as the Palm Desert Woman's Club and began its monthly luncheon meetings at the Shadow Mountain Club. Its continuing community project was to secure a public library, and in 1958, under the presidency of Mrs. Carl Henderson, it made an initial contribution of $3500 to the new community library board. The Woman's Club continues to contribute generously to scholarships and other projects for community benefit.

The Shadow Mountain Palette Club, an organization of artists, organized in May, 1961, with Irene Felton and the late Thirza Schenk Williams as leaders. There were 180 members in 1971, many of whom sell their art at displays in the Palm Desert Racquet Club (formerly the Shadow Mountain Club). Activities include demonstrations by famous artists, educational field trips, and awarding of art scholarships (five $1000 awards in 1972). Erma Woody is the current president.

In November, 1948, residents interested in equestrian activities organized the Palm Desert Raiders, a name derived from the group's custom of "raiding" member refrigerators after early morning rides. Junior and senior groups rode horses every Saturday from November to May, and they rode in festival and rodeo parades held periodically throughout the valley. Believed to be the first organization in Palm Desert, the group named Carl Henderson its first "Guide."

Desert Beautiful, Inc., was organized by Mrs. Clifford Henderson in 1962 "to preserve the natural beauty of the Coachella Valley, both its desert lands and its developed areas, and to improve the appearance of the communities of the valley." Membership grew, and the activities of the association affected eleven communities of the valley from Palm Springs to Thermal. It has conducted educational programs, sponsored essay and poster contests, and presented annual awards for special achievement in its fields of interest. It has waged imaginative and aggressive campaigns to obtain county, state, and federal aid in roadside trash collection, to promote appropriate plantings of native shrubs and trees, and to reduce visual pollution by roadside billboards.

For years before Desert Beautiful became active, Harry Oliver of Thousand Palms was a campaigner for roadside cleanup; through his publications his scorn of desert vandals and litter-bugs made its mark.

In 1954 a group of women residents formed a unit of Panhellenic, a national organization of university sororities. The group, now grown to seventy-five members, sponsors annual college scholarships which it awards to women graduates of valley high schools. Mrs. Edward C. Ruge, who worked with her late husband for many years to supervise the annual art show at the Date Festival in Indio, was named the first president. Panhellenic has monthly luncheons at various locations.

In 1964 the Palm Desert chapter of People-to-People International received its charter. Michael Faraday was the first president. The group assists in a national Hi-School Ambassador program, which sends young people on study trips to foreign countries; 1127 students from many communities made trips in 1970. James T. Doty, who was president of the Palm Desert Chamber of Commerce in 1964-65, was persuaded by President Eisenhower to take a major interest in the program. Doty helped organize the Palm Desert chapter, became director of the program in the western states, and in 1969 became international president of People-to-People.

When interest in theatricals waned, the Palm Desert Players disbanded, and its 4000-square foot Little Theater building at the south end of Willow Street was purchased in 1970 by the Coachella Valley Recreation and Parks District to be developed as a community center. In July, 1971, the Ahmanson Company donated to the District thirty acres adjoining the building, stipulating that the site be used for Palm Desert youth activities. Plans were immediately made to provide recreation and crafts programs and for additional development of the area.

The Palm Desert Junior Chamber of Commerce (Jaycees) was organized in 1963 with Robert Ricciardi as its first president. The twenty-five members meet twice monthly at the Indian Wells Hotel. It has sponsored projects for retarded children and a "peewee" ball team, has taken special interest in the creation and operation of a community recreation park.

The Palm Desert Community Park Foundation, Inc. was organized May 2, 1969, electing Mike Buccino president. Organizers included representatives of eleven civic organizations, constituting a foundation board of trustees. Its first discussions concerned locating appropriate sites and raising funds to acquire and develop them. Two years later the gift of thirty acres by the H. F. Ahmanson Company to the Coachella Valley Recreation and Park District partially satisfied the foundation's immediate quest. Don Shayler of the Jaycees succeeded Buccino as president in 1971, and he urged study of a possible outdoor amphitheater at the upper end of the Ahmanson grant and the securing of adequate baseball facilities at local school grounds.

There are seven Girl Scout troops in Palm Desert, and two Club Estates, comprising a membership of 59 Brownies,

84 Juniors, and 12 Cadets. Each group, under adult leadership, engages in various handicraft projects for community organizations. Mrs. Chris Landy is the neighborhood chairman.

Boy Scout Troop 76 was organized in 1948 with the Rotary Club as sponsor. Robin Barrett has been scoutmaster for the last five years. There are currently 32 boys in the troop, including five who hold the top Eagle rank. The troop has produced 23 Eagle Scouts since it was formed. Troop 88, organized later, meets at Lincoln School, and Ken Calkins is the scoutmaster. Bob Davis is cubmaster of Cub Pack 131, for boys 8 to 11 years of age.

With an initial membership of twenty-one women, the Soroptimist Club of Palm Desert was chartered in 1963, with Mrs. Jean Hanousek Butts as the first president. The club meets regularly to promote high standards in business and professional life, to advance the status of women, and to contribute to international understanding.

A Garden Club of the Desert was formed in May, 1963, with Mrs. Carl Henderson as president. It meets monthly to discuss the landscaping and planting of private yards, and to award a scholarship each year to a promising horticulture student at the College of the Desert. A second garden club was formed in 1970 with Mrs. T.J. Bluechel as president. Both groups do constructive work in beautifying local homes and gardens.

George Roy, publisher of an early paper, *The Resorter*, organized the Palm Desert Booster Club in 1948, assisted in reorganizing it in 1955 to become a local unit of the National Chamber of Commerce. Hal Kapp and Phil Franklin helped to organize the Chamber; Kapp has been an active director since the start. Lou Kuehner, present manager of the Retarded Children's Foundation, was an early secretary of the Chamber, followed by Don McNeilly. Joan Wyman served as Chamber secretary for seven years until her retirement in 1971. Kapp, as president in 1956-60, launched a campaign to force the two competing telephone companies to modify their rates. Public Utility Commission hearings required sixteen days with testimony from representatives of all the cove communities, resulting in directives permitting toll-free local use of phones. The Chamber worked to get the College of the Desert located in Palm Desert and it staged a prolonged drive to get news media to use a Palm Desert date-line on events initiated here (instead of Palm Springs). Membership in the Chamber in recent years has ranged between 200 and 300.

The Palm Desert Property Owners Association, interested primarily in zoning and taxation of property in the area, has been active since the early 1950s. Early in 1971 a group identified as Concerned Citizens of Palm Desert, claimed to have signed up 2,000 members within a few weeks. Concerned Citizens has declared its concern for orderly development, with consideration of population density, traffic patterns, and compatibility with acceptable standards in construction.

The three organizations mentioned above have frequently provided spokesmen for public hearings and civic discussions on subjects concerned with the town's residential and commercial development. The observer has some difficulty in choosing any one that "speaks for Palm Desert."

The Bank of America was the first financial institution to set up offices in Palm Desert, leasing temporary space in the original *Desert* Magazine building. It now has a modern building facing on Highway 111. Security Pacific Bank built its modern structure in the commercial area in the late 1950s. Pomona First Federal Savings and Loan Association has operated a Palm Desert office for several years. Santa Fe Federal Savings and Loan applied early this year for a permit to establish a branch to be located at the new Palms-to-Pines shopping center.

As indicated earlier in this chapter, it would be unsafe, irrelevant, and probably impossible to identify all the first retail establishments in Palm Desert. It is possible, however, to generalize with the observation that virtually every sales and service outlet available in a modern city may be found now in Palm Desert—with broader choices than are apparent in most cities of this size.

The barren cove has indeed become a flourishing community— and it all began with a print shop. I've heard of a town that started around a barrel of water (Steve Ragsdale's Desert Center), and others that had their beginnings in a livery stable or a country store, but not until I had witnessed the phenomena of Palm Desert had I seen a city grow around a Linotype machine. That this modest beginning became headquarters of a successful and influential regional magazine, a modern graphic arts establishment, and a distinguished art gallery is testimony to the vision and energy of one man, a man who saw beauty in this place and chose to make it the scene of his fulfillment.

N Allen

9. To Preserve and Protect

The Desert Protective Council and other conservation organizations provided mediums for the editor's talents.

AS NOTED in chapter six, in the early 1930s I steered 'Ol' Breezy' out of Calexico to historic or scenic places near Imperial Valley: Imperial Sand Hills, Tumco and Picacho Peak, Yuba Basin and Mount Signal, Painted Gorge and Coyote Mountains, the Anza and Butterfield Trails, Mecca Hills and Kofa of Arizona, and many other interesting spots. Most of these places showed few signs of recent visitation; some were virgin and few offered access roads. A striking contrast is a federal BLM-NPS study of 1968 which showed that there were 4.9 million visitor days recorded to the public lands of the California deserts that year, and predicted there would be 29.3 million visitors to the same areas by 1980. Annual visitor use for recreation in the Imperial Sand Hills alone is now 16,400 vehicles and 57,000 visitors.

Randall and I explored all the Borrego Badlands, Coyote Canyon, and the palm oases of eastern San Diego County at a time when we rarely saw wheel marks in the sand. Now the Anza-Borrego Desert State Park is a Mecca for thousands of visitors a year.

In the last forty years we have seen the Los Angeles metropolitan area become an urban nightmare with its unmanageable smog and congestion. Its residents, seeking respite, needed open space, clean air, clean water, and places where they could clear their minds of too much city and too many people. They found these treasured things in the desert, and they came back to enjoy it again and again.

An important reason for founding *Desert* Magazine in 1937 was our recognition of increasing interest in the desert. But we were almost a decade ahead of our time. After the war technological developments and increasing affluence changed the lives of city-bound people. Air conditioning for cars and homes made high temperatures tolerable, and four-wheel-drive vehicles made remote places accessible. On weekends from October to April the number of desert-bound campers exceeded the number that had formerly turned toward nearby mountain and beach resorts.

The phenomenal growth of demand for recreation in the desert areas of southern California is a societal change we could not have imagined forty years ago. It has created new problems which can be partially understood by quoting a few paragraphs from "The California Desert," a 378-page document published in 1968 by the California office of the

Bureau of Land Management and the western regional office of the National Park Service:

"From the Sierra Nevada and Death Valley, the California desert stretches south 240 miles to the border of Mexico. From the Colorado River it rolls west more than a hundred miles to touch the borders of Los Angeles.... sixteen million acres of starkly beautiful land, filled with a multitude of wonders; from sea-level sagebrush flats to range after range of high desert mountains, the California desert is ours to use— or to destroy.

"This is not some never-never land on the edge of the world; it literally lies within minutes of ten million people. And the smog-shrouded people who live in ticky-tacky box dwellings beside teeming freeways pour out upon the desert at every opportunity to play and rest and breath and stretch their arms. They seek the healing power of open land.

"People come, and they bring their box-like houses and beer cans and smog— and even their freeways— with them. They come to stay, and they chew away at the edge of the desert, often destroying the very thing they sought in the first place.

"Unfortunately, the desert seems boundless. It is so big that there appears to be room for everyone, and everything. Because of this illusion, our nation has played tic-tac-toe for the last hundred years with much of the California desert region. The land is scarred with road and utility rights-of -way, pockmarked by speculative mining operations, dese-crated by substandard construction, littered by trash and debris, and plundered of its natural and scenic values.

"The desert is limited; its resources are exhaustible. The ecological balance is fragile: soils, plants, animals, water, and air can be damaged for decades— or destroyed by thoughtless exploitation.

"Land management is now a problem and a challenge,

not only of managing the lands themselves, but of managing the people who use them. As a people we must make decisions soon to determine how we will use these arid lands so that they will best provide for us and for those that come after us."

This is an eloquent plea for the marriage of recreation and conservation, but forcing that union will not be easy. We are now seeing recreation as the thoughtless youth who roars his dune buggy through verbena fields in the sandhills or scrawls his name across the face of ancient Indian pictographs. We are seeing conservation as the thoughtful young woman who cautions, "Let us leave it unspoiled so that others may enjoy this place, or so we may return to enjoy it again." Not all recreationists are thoughtless, but the number of despoilers is multiplying so rapidly their thirst for the wine of freedom will destroy themselves, their conservative companions, and the open space itself. If the parties shun the vows of fidelity, society must hold the shotgun which forces the marriage, and it must prescribe the rules of conduct which will assure compatibility. As any counselor knows, a voluntary and joyful embrace is a better way to assure happiness.

Editor Henderson found his recreation—alone or with a few friends—long before the deserts were inundated by people. In fact, he made it his business to draw people to the deserts— and business improved. But Randall realized, perhaps better than other thoughtful men of his time, that the desert was a fragile thing and that it could be destroyed unless he did what he could to protect and preserve it. Randall may have unknowingly encouraged "free lance" recreation by his own example, but he became increasingly aware of the dangers of uncontrolled use of the public domain. Long before ecology became a standard word in contemporary language he was drawing attention to vandalism of historical monuments and archeological remains, unnecessary expansion of training and bombing areas by the armed forces, and the lethargy of legislators regarding protection of plant and animal life on desert lands.

In 1947 Randall Henderson was elected an Honorary Vice President of the Sierra Club "in recognition of his efforts to acquaint the public with the values of deserts through his writings and publications." Francis Farquhar, the pioneer Sierra Club president who made the nomination, said he believed Randall was "a sincere conservationist in the true Sierra Club tradition." This was twenty years before environmental legislation became top news.

On May 11, 1970 (less than two months before Randall's death), Raymond J. Sherwin, secretary of the Sierra Club, wrote to Randall: "It is with great pleasure that I have the privilege of informing you officially of your re-election as Honorary Vice President of the Sierra Club..... I suspect that this news is not altogether unexpected, but I think we all experience a warm feeling of gratification to be reminded of our association with you." Randall's reply expressed appreciation for the honor bestowed on him by this great national organization for 23 years, adding: "What a satisfying thing it is to be a veteran conservationist in these days when an entire nation—and perhaps all the civilized world—is being awakened to the critical importance of preserving our planetary environment."

His *Desert* editorials on conservation, although lacking the poetry and passion of John Muir in earlier crises, were thoughtful and reasoned, and they were strong on facts. His quiet crusade began to get attention, especially where it counted among bureaucrats and law-makers. But he needed to join his voice with others, and he found that opportunity in 1954.

A small group of conservation-minded people of southern California met in September, 1954, to discuss desert problems in connection with the programs of the Conservation Forum of the Trailfinders.* They agreed that an organization was needed to concentrate its interests in desert areas, and a five-member committee was named to work on the matter. Henderson was a member of the committee, and he supplied many of the names for the invitational mailing which went out before the end of the month. An organizational meeting was held around a blazing fire of desert driftwood the evening of October 23 in the mouth of Deep Canyon; more than forty people responded to the invitations.

The campfire group agreed to organize, chose the name Desert Protective Council, and elected an executive board of seven (the board in turn elected Harry C. James, widely recognized leader in conservation activities, as its first president). Although the immediate goal of the Council was to preserve the integrity of California's Joshua Tree National Monument, it adopted a statement of purposes much broader in impact:

"The purposes of the Desert Protective Council shall be to safeguard for wise and reverent use by this and succeeding generations those desert areas that are of unique scenic, scientific, historical, spiritual, and recreational value, and to educate, by all appropriate means, children and adults to a better understanding of the desert in order that the objectives of the Council may be attained."

The Joshua Tree National Monument, on the north rim of Coachella Valley, was facing threats from mining and highway interests. During the next few years the Council sought and obtained support for its position, and succeeded

---

* Trailfinders was founded by Harry C. James of Banning in 1914. One of the projects of the outdoor organization was to take boys on outings to New Mexico and Arizona, often led by Charles Fletcher Lummis, famous editor of *Out West*. Randall Henderson became a member of Trailfinders' advisory council soon after the founding of *Desert* Magazine, and he sponsored and led groups of boys on trips to the palm canyons of southern California.

in blocking immediate commercial exploitation of the Monument.

With other organizations it crusaded successfully against mining operations in Tucson Mountain Park, opposed construction of Echo Park Dam in Dinosaur National Monument, sought legislative protection in California for bighorn sheep, desert tortoise, and ringtail cat; kept a graded road out of Coyote Canyon of Anza-Borrego State Park, stopped the cutting of ironwood near Wiley Well for charcoal, limited military land acquisition to 5,000 acres without Congressional approval, and helped to create the National Wilderness Preservation System.

Randall, in his *Desert* editorials and later in his work with the Council's *El Paisano,* had long opposed hunting of wild life in the desert, and he pressed his views in the Council. Although he had observed the strong lobbying activity of sportsman organizations in opposing restrictive legislation, he was surprised to find similar resistance among his conservationist associates. It took him several years to obtain endorsement of resolutions against the killing of mourning dove, bighorn sheep, and "the poisoning and trapping of the so-called predators and rodents and related government-sponsored uses of insecticides and herbicides." Here is one of the low-pitched comments he made on this subject:

"As far as I can recall, the Council as an organization has never adopted a policy involving the issue of game hunting versus no hunting. What I write on this page is an expression of personal opinion, but my long association with this organization has convinced me that DPC members generally may be classified in the 'no hunting' category."

He cited the example of a man and his wife who had rallied influential support for their campaign to stop the poisoning of coyotes in the Chuckawalla and Chocolate Mountains. The man found out that there had been no lamb killing by marauders in recent years and that the federal Predator Control Act men had been working on records that were valid five years previously. He obtained a promise that the poisoned bait would be removed immediately. He wrote to Randall, "Now Rose and I and our camping companions are looking forward again to a time when the kit foxes will be coming into our camp-outs for handouts, and we will again hear the serenade of the coyote chorus."

The editor preceded this anecdote with this comment: "The role of the conservationist is often a lonely one. The problems are many, and often complex. All about us we see an urgent need for action which would preserve the things and the values we regard as essential to human survival on this planet.

"We are deeply aware of the brutal destruction of wildlife, the needless despoliation of the virgin landscape, the thoughtless desecrations of the litterbug, the cupidity of those whose god is the golden idol of profit, and perhaps most distressing of all, the apathy of a citizenship too engrossed with immediate personal problems to have acquired any sense of fellowship with or reverence for the natural elements of our planetary environment.

"We sometimes feel a sense of frustration, and the question recurs: 'What can I do to help solve these problems?'"

Desert Protective Council incorporated July 13, 1955, and the incorporators were Harry C. James, Mrs. Ralph H. Lutz, Richard M. Keller, Henry W. Weber MD, Randall Henderson, Roderick Leap, Don Luis Percival, Ernest R. Tinkham, and Ronald L. Johnson. Written into the bylaws and articles of incorporation was a provision for creation of an educational foundation. Funds received by the foundation were held separately and were used "to sponsor publication of educational material relative to the aims of the Council," to encourage educational programs in various media, conduct lectures, field trips, and similar activities. Under California law the Council is prohibited from educational activities aimed at influencing legislation or participating in campaigns on behalf of candidates seeking political offices.

At the 1972 election of officers, the Council chose four women for leadership positions, headed by Mrs. John C. (Helen) Dengler. Backing her up are Mrs. Joe Read, vice president; Mrs. Jane S. Pinheiro, treasurer; and Mrs. Karen Fowler, secretary. The new president has a formidable record of professional and civic activities to her credit: assistant director and public relations for Student's International Travel Association (SITA) for 33 years, chairman of the Riverside County Park Advisory Commission, coordinator of Desert Beautiful, founder of the Order of the Bighorn Society of White Sun Guest Ranch, board of governors of Living Desert Association, and member of seven other community planning or environmental organizations.

Mrs. Dengler announced that a continuing project of the Council will be emphasized this year: the acquisition by gift or purchase of some 1700 parcels of privately-held land in Anza-Borrego Desert State Park. As the land becomes available—to be identified as "memory gardens"—the new acreage will be turned over to the state park system in order to make possible an orderly development of the public parkland.

Membership of the council is approximately 700, with an additional thirty-nine distinguished authors, conservationists, educators, and scientists serving on its advisory panel. An observation of the current membership list suggests that a large percentage have passed a normal retirement age, and active participation is thus minimized. Executive Director Bob Bear believes that involvement of professional leadership and enrollment of younger people is necessary in order to enlarge future programs.

A major sponsorship of the foundation has been publication of a quarterly newsletter for members (with a small subscription price for interested non-members). The first president, Harry James, was persuaded by his executive board to assume the role of executive director, a volunteer position, a role he ably filled until 1961, when he took an extended trip to Europe. Robert G. Bear of Beaumont, semi-retired accountant and purchasing agent and an active Sierra Clubber, was elected acting executive secretary at that time (dropping the "acting" in 1964), a post he continues to fill to the present. As part of his function, James founded and edited the quarterly *El Paisano* (the road runner). Normally eight to sixteen pages, the publication contained articles and letters by Council consultants, as well as pictures and news notes.

After Randall's retirement from *Desert*, he frequently contributed editorials and book reviews to the publication, produced five issues in 1962, and held the editorship from 1965 through 1969 (a total of twenty-five issues).

In his non-salaried role as editor of *El Paisano*, Randall studied the growing volume of conservation literature which flooded his mail, reported the basic ideas in the new ecology-oriented books, and carried on a prodigious correspondence with legislators and friends of the Council's objectives. He had been a member of the Council's executive board from the beginning and he spent much time participating in committee meetings, assisting in arrangements for meetings, and escorting influential citizen groups to desert sites involved in Council projects.

For a man who had passed his 77th birthday at the time he accepted the editorship of the quarterly, his product had an unexpected vitality and perception, although many of his editorial pages leaned heavily on quotations from authors of relevant subjects. The range of his interest in desert subjects is suggested in a brief review of some of *El Paisano's* issues.

His last editorial was on population control, a subject he

touched frequently in his final years. He observed that "The thoughtful among us have become awakened to the fact that this planet earth is a fragile thing. For too long generations of Americans have subscribed to the notion that growth and expansion are virtues, that nature must be subdued, that wilderness is idle land that must be put to use, that everything that makes a buck is good. But a new concept is gaining acceptance, the realization that growing population and advancing technology have created problems which have become a threat to the health and security of present and future generations of human beings. We are learning about the science of ecology, the dependence of man on his environment, and of all forms of life on each other."

In 1967 he reviewed Robert Train Rienow's *Moment in the Sun* and several other books on the deteriorating quality of the American environment, and he concluded that the logical answer to the problems of pollution was to institute sweeping government controls on disposal of all waste.

A few months later he reviewed Paul R. Ehrlich's *Population Bomb,* suggesting that the concept of too many people was a question of special interest "to all people who are committed to a continuing effort in behalf of conservation of our planet's natural resources.

"You and I and others who are aligned with us in conservation activities are seeking to preserve as much as possible of our wilderness areas. We don't want our landscapes cluttered with billboards. We are opposed to pollution of air and water. We seek to protect all wild life and to preserve the fertility of our soil. We pass resolutions and write letters to Congressmen. We protest the building of dams in Grand Canyon, and we try to save as many acres as we can of the redwood forests for future generations to enjoy. Much of the time we are on the defensive. Much of our effort is to preserve against the selfishness or greed of those who would consume or destroy."

Three E's were repeated themes during Randall's editorship of the Council quarterly: ecology, evolution, and education on the environment. Occasionally he added a fourth: emotion, although he seemed at a loss to define the power of feeling or to demonstrate it in his own life. A sample was: "Our men of science have done their job so well that we now have the capacity to produce ample food and shelter and provide adequate medical care and education for every American citizen. And yet our emotional life is so imperfect and so badly organized, we are so insensitive to the emotional values of love and compassion, that some of our people have more wealth than is good for them while millions of others live in poverty and ignorance."

On ecology, he observed that "my generation of students a half century ago went through school without ever hearing the word *ecology*. Today I regard it as one of the most important studies in the educational system..... The problems of balance on this earth can never be left to the judgment of men who have selfish interests at stake. I sincerely hope it is true today that man is beginning to behave as he must, as a living creature who depends on other life for his own existence."

He reported the ideas of speakers at the Biennial Wilderness Conference, and concluded that "Some of the most scholarly men in our nation have defined the new discipline which must be added to the curriculum in the school of conservation. We must continue to crusade in defense of the golden eagle and the tule elk, for unpolluted air and uncontaminated water, for wild unobstructed rivers and virgin forests. But our mission must also include in capital letters the concept of SPACE, space in which humans may live and work and worship unhampered by the inevitable distractions of an overcrowded population."

An interest which consumed much of Randall's time from

1962 to 1969 was the setting aside of public lands as natural areas, largely through executive action of the Bureau of Land Management. His correspondence on this subject covered areas throughout the desert southwest, particularly in Riverside County. He exerted special effort on a 23-section site in the Santa Rosa Mountains, to be withdrawn from mining claims and occupancy for the protection of the bighorn sheep range. Centering on the upper Dead Indian Canyon, the area is a checkerboard of public and private lands. On petition of six conservation organizations last year, BLM began proceedings to declare the area natural reserve and to attempt to trade property in order to make public ownership contiguous.

Robert Bear commented on Randall's contributions: "His dominant personality gave him an influential role in shaping DPC policies until his death. As editor of *El Paisano* he brought heightened prestige through his forceful, lucid expressions of DPC positions. His editorials effectively expressed his opinions, particularly regarding the welfare of American Indians."

At the annual meeting of the Desert Protective Council four months after Henderson's death, Harry James delivered a memorial address, concluding with:

"From the day that Randall was our chief sponsor and host at the organizational meeting of this Council, he not only served on its board of directors but to a very large extent he was the Council's mentor and guide. All of us who served with him came to appreciate the extent of his knowledge and dedication to the deserts of the southwest. He seemed to have been everywhere. We could not mention a palm grove, a spring, or a spectacular viewpoint but that Randall had camped there. Whenever the Council needed money his checkbook was always ready.

"Randall was an impatient man, but during many a drawn-out meeting he curbed his impatience in order to see the matter through if it in any way helped in the preservation of the deserts. He drove himself hard, and he expected others to do the same.

"It pleased him to see his efforts—and those of the Council—come to fruition in a wide-spread appreciation of the desert. Frequently these gains came as the result of compromise. Although Randall hated to compromise, when he did it is interesting to note that nearly all such compromises were decidedly slanted to justify his original viewpoint.

"A fitting memorial to Randall Henderson's achievement in years to come will be whispered by those who visit the dozens of national parks, monuments, and state and county parks that Randall did so much to establish and maintain 'for wise and reverent use by this and succeeding generations.'"

10. A Vision of A Utopian Tomorrow

Editor Henderson had deep
convictions regarding man's
social and economic condition.

FEW OF US can define precisely what our political stance
is, or how we got there. Definitions of radical, liberal, moderate, conservative— or shades in between— are usually vague,

or at least they are vague in the mind of the man who tries to pin-point his personal beliefs about major political issues. Randall Henderson was never vague about specific politicians or the issues they espoused, but he was reticent about tagging himself with a generalization about party loyalty. I take the liberty, then, of defining my old friend as I saw him, particularly in his later years: a middle-class liberal, tending toward radical views. He would not have thought the tag particularly important or relevant, but I attach it to explain the evolution of his thinking and his eagerness in planning for a time when he could expand his study of political, economic, and religious philosophy.

When I first knew Randall forty years ago he was a registered Republican; he supported Hoover mildly, but was enthusiastic about Wendell Wilkie. He was never quite sure about Franklin Roosevelt, but he applauded most of his national recovery programs. He admired the writings and speeches of Adlai Stevenson, but he voted for Eisenhower. He abhorred the antics of Joe McCarthy, the implications of the John Birch Society, and the threats of George Wallace. When I wrote him in 1969 that I had switched my registration from Republican to Democrat, he responded that he had done the same five years earlier.

Economics interested him far more than did politics. His interest in national and state campaigns usually centered in the economic issues, and this interest continued in county and municipal administrations in areas in which he worked. In his private life he was a conservative in money matters; he had known the meaning of austerity. Middle-class liberals are ambivalent about property. They are comfortable with their things and couldn't get along without them, but social passions and idealism make them ashamed of ownership, and especially the love of ownership. This was true of Henderson. When he no longer had the financial problems of building and operating his properties he could shake off his shame and give his attention to the problems which he felt were afflicting the nation and the world.

During his newspaper career Henderson did not attempt roles as political pundit or economic expert, except on a limited scale concerning local issues. As editor of *Desert* Magazine he rarely editorialized on money matters except as they might apply to desert living, and they were invariably secondary to the ideals expressed in his original editorial policy.

Before we founded *Desert* Magazine Randall was deeply concerned with the 1930 depression. He read the liberal columnists, including Upton Sinclair and Herbert Agar; studied the works of Ortega y Gasset and Petr Kropotkin, and followed the public statements of the economic brain-trusters. Years later he wrote me—during his military service in the Sahara— that he was getting some of his own ideas down on paper. When we were together during the decade following the war we had vigorous arguments about some of the national issues which concerned him, particularly in the field of public education, on which I could speak with some authority because of my employment with a large teacher association.

On passing his 65th year, Randall became restive about finding a manager for his publishing enterprise, because he wanted more time to work on "The Book." It was a great relief to him when he sold the magazine, as well as the real estate and improvements of the Palm Desert enterprise, in September 1958. He began work at once on what he hoped would be the final drafts of his socio-economic manuscript.

In the summer of 1960 he traveled to New York to talk with book editors in some of the major publishing houses. On July 26 he wrote me that he had left the manuscript with Knopf "and I expect an answer in five or six weeks."

The next year he published "On Desert Trails, Yesterday and Today," and he was immensely pleased with the meticulous production by Paul Bailey at Westernlore Press in Eagle Rock. I had long urged him to direct his energies to a subject where he had no peer: his experience in the deserts of the southwest. It pleased me when he dedicated the book to me and other companions of desert expeditions. Then followed a long silence about "The Book;" apparently the publisher's response had not been encouraging.

In April, 1964, he wrote: "The manuscript of the book I finished immediately after I retired was rejected by Alfred Knopf. I've learned the reason why: no publisher will accept an authoritative non-fiction book written by John Doe of Nebraska.... I must write my story as fiction. Hence I have retained the services of a literary consultant, who has promised to coach me in the fine art of the dramatist. Can you imagine me, with forty years of experience as a tough old reporter, dealing in romance and poetry?"

Randall's widow told me there was another reason for rejection: the big publishers will not take on an aged writer with no previous success in book titles; they would have no opportunity to promote his name for future exposure to the public. Unfortunately, this was a merchandising factor that Randall had ignored.

More than a year later he wrote "I have begun a complete revision of the book I told you about a long time ago." Apparently he was laboring with the transition of his work into fiction form. He also wrote at length about his impressions of churches, churchmen, and religion, without direct reference to Christian doctrine. He had been attracted to a Unitarian church by the minister's attitudes on science. He had been a member of the Center for the Study of Democratic Institutions at Santa Barbara from its beginning, and he found great satisfaction in listening to discourses between learned men at the conference hall. He quoted from the liberal periodicals; he was a subscriber to *Saturday Review, The Progressive,* and other liberal magazines.

"I am still plodding along on the book," he wrote in May, 1965. "With the world involved in revolutionary change, the writing of a Utopian book in this period is really a tough challenge, but the reading and study involved certainly is an interesting occupation for a retired printer with no financial worries." He had decided to title the book "In the Sunlight of Tomorrow." No doubt running through his mind were the kinds of questions later posed by Peter Schrag in *Saturday Review* (March 25, 1972): "What kinds of cohesive possibilities exist for a nation that must give up its historic dreams? Should someone be saying that the future of the country does not lie in material stuff or in world dominance but in major political, social, and cultural reforms premised on the idea that the old assumptions won't work, that resources and power must be reallocated, and that all the economic measures of the past few years have done little more than enlarge corporate profits and concentrate even more in corporate institutions?"

A year after Randall's death I read the complete 327-page typewritten manuscript of the unpublished work. It is not my function here to praise or condemn the work, but rather to describe its content and treatment as an illustration of the idealistic thought which moved the author. Randall would probably have described himself as a "pragmatic idealist." We find him almost from the start admonishing his characters toward "hard work and intensive study," and reminding them that they will reach their goals through "objective thinking."

The narrative opens with introduction of a young male student entering a midwestern college. The son of African missionaries, he had spent most of his life on the dark continent. He had the usual adjustments to student life on campus, including professorial orientation to a moral life. The college president lectures through most of the first chapter on the theme that "there are many rooms in our lives, but we close the doors." An economics professor then carries on with his definition of communism, his questioning of the *laissez faire* principle, and his doubts about the stability of the American monetary system. Here is a portion of his discourse:

"While inflation at home, shrinkage of foreign markets, and automation are three of the main factors in bringing about the low ebb of the American economy today, other influences are at work. We are in a period of transition. We are trying to maintain the illusion that we still have the free enterprise system which served our forefathers well over a hundred years ago, in an age when advances in communication, transportation, invention, and science have completely transformed the environment in which we work. The older generation is clinging tenaciously to a theory which became obsolete when farmers were granted subsidies, and most of the population was placed under the protective umbrella of social security legislation. I am not saying these subsidies and benefits are wrong; I am merely pointing out that they are the deeds of a planned economy, and not a free economy as conceived by Adam Smith.

"It remains for the men and women of your generation and mine to find the answers, and we shall seek earnestly to do so, keeping always in mind that here in America we respect and must preserve the dignity and the integrity of the individual citizen."

The economic theory is sound (if that maligned "science" can be judged only in historical terms), the platitudes are evenly spaced, and the contemporary U.S. history is impeccable. But unfortunately, the words of all the speakers— page after page of quoted paragraphs— are all Henderson's words, all the same vocabulary and structure no matter whether they come out of the mouths of student, minister, college president, or professor. This mars the reader's sense of identification, but it also points accurately toward the author's basic thinking. And that, after all, is the purpose of this chapter.

The author then traces the growth of fascism in this country, and he finds it destructive. His characters talk about the growing dangers of inflation, and they tend to blame the super-corporations and the Wall Street money-masters. Solution of these problems must come, of course, out of the right thinking of the younger generation. The All Nations Student League is organized for active participation in national politics. The chief character becomes a leader of the organization, and he sets out "to make a new and better world, without violence or sophistry."

Our student takes a summer job at a national park where he hears a ranger lecture on ecology. Here we sample Randall's consuming interest: illustrations of natural balance in life cycles, and the urgent need to preserve these balances for man's survival.

We return to a long discussion of the conflict between competitive enterprise and cooperative enterprise, with a questioning of the struggle concept advanced in Darwinian theory. The author draws a conclusion that competitive man is obsolete. The "Under-Privileged Consumer" requires a chapter, with elementary lessons in economics, complete with abhorrence of an unbalanced budget and a rising national debt.

The country moves into a new depression, with soup kitchens, money problems, and low public morale. There is a sensational offer by the Chinese to disarm their atomic weapons and place themselves under U.N. control (this was written six years before Red China was admitted to the United Nations). Economic woes are compounded by collapse of the stock market on defense industry issues. The electorate revolts, the student congress forms a Third Party and issues a 21-plank platform, largely based on economic reform. A liberal governor speaks to the youth congress and, among other things, denounces "progressive" education. The governor becomes a candidate, and his campaign speeches are heavily laden with moral overtones, urging the overthrow of monopolies. Elected to the Presidency, the leader espouses a theme of "faith to live by," proceeds to revise the monetary system, gearing the money supply to production. A result is the rapid growth of consumer cooperative societies.

Biological sciences and the use of languages are emphasized in classrooms, "life adjustment" disappears (at least as a descriptive phrase). There are courses in applied psychology, which are identified as "the art of objective thinking." The author makes it clear that the new society will avoid forcing the individual into conforming roles.

We have covered 279 pages when the author causes the young student, now a retired doctor with long professional service in Africa, returning to America (in the year 2015) to find his "restoration of faith." The United States is cleaner, the people relaxed and happy. There is no pollution, no billboards to mar the scenery, hospitality centers are conspicuous in every town. There is a heavy tax on radio and television and a regimentation of programming. Cooperative societies dominate the economic system by unifying the demands of consumers. The book ends with a pastor-naturalist speaking in a wilderness setting on a theme of "reverence for the things of God's creation."

The manuscript is an acceptable economics text, with strong overtones of social idealism. The "good guys" march through its pages, preaching with unswerving solemnity, showing no signs of character vulnerability. The "bad guys" apparently remain behind locked doors on which vague labels appear; they never charge out for confrontation, or even to defend the status quo. At stage center conflict never raises its ugly head. There is cold logic in Henderson's narrative, but it is the logic of the idealist who refuses to examine the erosion of human character or to accept the reality of open conflict in effecting change. But my critique of the book's design serves no useful purpose except to reveal the thinking of the writer.

Several questions have bothered me through the years: Why did Randall Henderson invest so much of his life in a private search for his Utopia? What ends could he hope to gain beyond an ephemeral hope that he could deter mankind from plunging into even deeper whirlpools of stupidity and blind serfdom? Was it pessimism or optimism that directed his thinking? I have no solid answers; I can only guess.

Randall was essentially a pragmatist, he wanted to know whether it would work, whether a new proposal would conform to practical experience. But in the back of his brain was a large section of idealism, of belief that the greatest good would triumph if one worked at it sensibly. He placed much faith in the rule of reason, and he assumed that most men are similarly motivated.

Harry Ashmore, president of the Center for the Study of Democratic Institutions (of which Randall was for three years a founding member), wrote an essay about the liberal, who "recognizes that, in his own time at least, the ideal is impossible to attain, and that his primary task may be to see that the necessary compromises are not fatal." Ashmore then adds:

"While the liberal's own history has made him skeptical of the short-range results of democracy, he sees no substitute for self-government as the only feasible check on the managerial and scientific/technological elites required for the functioning of an advanced society. He acknowledges the existence of power, and distrusts it; he accepts the use of force only when it is applied with constituted authority and the rule of law; he puts his ultimate trust in the capacity of men to reconcile their differences without coercion if society can be made to approximate Thomas Jefferson's free marketplace of ideas.... Tolerance is the liberal's cardinal virtue, and he cherishes civility as the literal and essential derivation of civilization."

Ashmore's definition is an approximation of Randall's state of mind and his willingness to concentrate on a pattern which he hoped would fit his better society. It would probably apply to his hope that Palm Desert, springing almost before his eyes out of the virgin desert, would become an ideal social structure, untainted by the ills he saw in society.

Putting tags on people can be misleading or false, since few of us are expert in defining the characteristics of the human mind. The botanist finds it useful to identify genus and species in his study of plant life, and that is possible because he works with absolutes. But the thinking man of the mid-twentieth century, in considering the social condition, did not have the positive and the unquestionable as his bulwarks. His own life experience had taught him that forces beyond his control sought to corrupt him, and he hoped that compassion, justice, integrity, and charity were still alive.

Randall wanted to change and improve the society in which he lived, not by revolution but by reasonable acceptance of alternatives. For the last quarter of his life I submit that he was a liberal in the best sense. The tag fits.

— x x x —

RANDALL had done a lot of thinking about the "tomorrow" of his own town, Palm Desert, and he obviously had this in mind when he wrote a page of copy which I found in his files. He had labeled it "Tomorrow" and this sentence followed: "One of the privileges of authorship is to indulge in fantasy. I therefore presume that this chapter might be entitled

"Adventures in Wishful Thinking," for it will be just that." A brief introduction, together with numerous guide-posts in his files, suggested the route he would have taken had he been able to put his "adventures" on paper. I presume to carry on as though the following paragraphs had come out of his typewriter.

The year is 1990. We are seated high on a mountain overlooking a spacious desert cove; the rocky slopes above the sandy floor seem to be barren and uninviting. Only the dark green of the coniferous forest lying at high levels of the mountain provides clues to the effect of temperature and rainfall on the proliferation of living things.

We look down on the green oasis of Palm Desert, with its parks and open spaces, its wide streets and tidy home gardens. This gently sloping bajada was once called barren; only the lowly creosote bush and smoke tree seemed to thrive. There was only one weathered shack on the land nearly fifty years ago when a few dreamers talked of founding a community here. Thirty years later the assessed valuation of the area was estimated at $65 million. An acre that a man could have bought then for a day of labor would now cost him a year or more of labor in order to own it.

In 1968 there were fewer than 8,000 people living in Palm Desert; there are more than 30,000 now. In all the cove communities from the Whitewater to the edge of Indio more than 80,000 people now make their homes.

I recall with pleasure that a large percentage of the first home-makers found a unique charm in this desert setting, something special which they wanted to preserve. They soon learned that the soil and the plant life on this sand could be easily destroyed, so they replanted and made their city green and beautiful. The surrounding mountain ranges were eternal, unchangeable, and the people saw no reason why they should not also have clean, sun-lit air eternally.

In time that idyllic belief was eroded due to technological changes created by burgeoning populations; the whole western world was finding out about the causes and cures of air pollution. Even in this Garden of Eden new dwellers could not escape some of the trauma of the time. The first signs were brown clouds creeping through San Gorgonio Pass. In the decade of the 30s we had not seen this phenomenon, although we knew occasional sand-storms which irritated our wives and gave us opportunity for self-indulgent conversation. The industrial and vehicular smog of the coastal area had invaded our Paradise, and we were helpless before it.

We could not stem the brown-cloud intrusion, but we could fight the installation of smog and dust producing plants in our own environment— and we raised effective barriers against that threat. We were thankful when the modification of internal combustion engines brought us relief from impending danger, and we are now seeing the beneficial result of this self-regimentation.

The spread of residential and commercial subdivisions near Indio made many date palm trees available for transplanting, and they became a conspicuous addition to the landscaping of Palm Desert. The transplanting of native desert trees and shrubs is prohibited by law, but nurserymen and home gardeners developed palo verde, desert willow, and even smoke tree stocks, and they were wisely used for home gardens. Dealers in cactus, yucca, and citrus trees found a ready market. It has been more than a generation since the first plantings were brought to this virgin cove, and they have made the city a place of beauty, in harmony with its environment.

As is typical of any new community composed of people having differing life habits, there was little unity in community planning during the first few years. Action groups worked toward the ends they believed to be the most important—

there were dozens of organizations in Palm Desert by 1970—
and fragmentation of effort seemed to be the standard condition. Any man who might suggest creation of a single coordinating agency in order to obtain a high degree of consensus
would be suspected of grinding his ax for his special purposes.

Residents who envisioned higher tax bills because of
increased public services vigorously fought those who wanted
to create a "model city." Somewhere between these two view-
points there had to be certain points of common interest, and
these points became visible as lax or nonexistent zoning and
building ordinances permitted construction generally believed
to approach "architectural monstrosity." Small discussion
groups began to talk about community values— real or potential, aesthetic or commercial— which affected the lives of all.
The influence of constructive thinkers was felt in the town,
and strong leadership came forward to unite the people for
effective action.

Abortive efforts to create an incorporated city had shaken
the community a half dozen times. Beginning in 1963 several
petition drives were thwarted by citizen apathy, and in 1970
voters rejected a proposal to incorporate an area of 38 square
miles. Finally, in 1975, a centralized local government was
established by a narrow voter margin.

Fortunately, five men of exceptional strength and
patience were elected to the first city council, and they gave
unstintingly of their time to bring about resolution of major
problems. They employed a municipal management staff that
provided adequate service at low cost; they set up procedures
which permitted townspeople to examine—and register their
opinions—regarding proposed building projects. The council
chambers became a central point for the abrogation of differences and a forum for the discussion of plans for community
development.

Twenty years ago the County proposed a general plan

which would affect all of the cove areas outside incorporated cities. Since then four cities have incorporated and the basic purposes of the general plan have been coordinated, particularly as it affected recreational and cultural facilities and the unification of water and sewage systems. With wise zoning and the use of advisory panels on planning and architecture, population density has been reduced in the over-all area, in spite of total population increase. There have been rigid controls on introduction of heavy industry as a step in controlling smog; erosion and smog control measures of various kinds have kept the air clean, and the mountain ranges have protected us from the relatively low levels of smog in coastal areas.

As I indicated earlier, tourism and recreation continue to be the basic economic foundations of the community. But fortunately the increase of leisure time for most families, as well as individual wealth, have made it possible for the community to maintain a continuing prosperity.

Large community parks, as well as neighborhood parks, wind breaks and vegetative ground cover, and green belts along the highways have preserved the oasis quality of the communities and have insured the maintenance of high environmental standards. The area's designation as "Golf Capitol of the World" continues to be the cornerstone of the "recreation industry." In addition, large areas of public land in nearby mountains have been set aside as wild life reserves and as refuge for bighorn sheep.

Led by a group of citizens who had sponsored the creation of the beautiful Palm Desert Cultural Arts Center on the campus of the College of the Desert, plans for the building of an amphitheater on the western slope at the edge of the city were consummated fifteen years ago. Among active supporters were the members of the Inter-Church Council, ably assisted by friends of the Living Desert Reserve and the College of the Desert. The site is a natural bowl having a backdrop of rocky hillside covered with a variety of desert plant life. Its seating area is connected to a large parking lot by short, winding paths which provide vantage points for views of the wide desert plane rimmed by distant mountains.

The dedication services of Desert Bowl were held on a brilliantly starlit evening in April, and every seat was occupied when the local symphony orchestra and choral group rendered musical compositions especially written for the occasion. Spotlights focused on the principal speaker, a noted minister with a reputation as a renowned naturalist-scientist. He made appropriate remarks about the beauty of the environment and praised the sponsors of the movement to create "this magnificent meeting-place under the stars." He then spoke in this fashion:

"The creature of the forest and field has only a physical destiny to fulfill: to grow and reproduce its kind and then vanish from the earth, leaving only the physical elements of his body as a contribution to the new cycle of life. Within limits the animal may adapt to a changing environment, but it leaves no tradition, no guidance for future generations of its kind.

"Man is an animal with something added, something very important. For inherent in every man is that spark—a divine spark if you prefer—which enables him to select the mode of his life, to mold his own character to similate the goal he envisions, and to make a positive contribution to those around him and those who come after him.

"One of the measures of man's maturity is the degree of his awareness, his capacity to accept responsibility for altruist responses to that still small voice inside him. While we cannot define the goal of evolutionary destiny, we can be sure that the voice of a chaste intuition will be a safe guide, a guide down the road of eager and unselfish quest for understanding of self, and this is God's greatest gift to man."

NAllen

11. Retrospect and Anecdote

Fragments of viewpoint and
observation may give depth to
this history/biography.

The trail of Desert Magazine, its origin, growth, transformation in a new environment, and its change of character under new ownerships, was littered with rocks and
thorny cactus. The stretches of hard, level sand showed
infrequently, but perhaps they gave renewed strength to
the few people who carried heavy packs up the difficult
slopes to the crests. The story of Desert is, of course, the
story of the inter-relationships of people, those who carried
the loads and those who encouraged them on, as well as

those who blocked the trail and decried the effort......
There were some fragments of the story about Randall
Henderson and the desert in which he lived that did not
seem to fit properly in this book, and I have saved these
anecdotes for this final section.

A DESERT LOVE STORY

LUCILE HARRIS was the first employee of *Desert* Magazine
(actually the only employee for a long time because the publishers drew no salaries). She came to our El Centro office in
the fall of 1937 after experience as a newspaper reporter,
feature writer, and columnist in the San Diego area. She
proved to be adaptable; she started with typing, proof reading,
and other clerical duties, but was soon handling the multiple
details of the circulation department. Competent and depend-
able, her work was meticulous and thoughtful. She was soon
handling correspondence in several departments: photo contests, poetry page, and news summaries, as well as assisting
in critical review of contributions. A small woman with a
broad forehead and large, luminous eyes and a pleasant,
low-keyed voice, she was a gracious receptionist when visitors
came to the office.

When Randall was called to active duty in World War II,
he left Lucile in charge as acting editor. She handled the desk
for two years until Randall's return in late 1944, and continued
to carry a heavy load of editorial work during construction of
the new plant at Palm Desert.

During the war she received communications from a
young man in the Army Air Forces, an instructor in radar
navigation, who submitted entries in the photo contests and
offered suggestions on historical subjects; he was obviously
well-informed on desert themes. He also ordered books by
mail which were shipped to his parents' home in Pasadena;
he had become a desert bibliophile. About the time of the
Japanese surrender in 1945 the young man, Harold Weight,

offered some suggestions which he thought might be appropriate for *Desert* coverage. Randall asked Lucile to find out whether the man had post-war plans. She laughingly said years later that her inquiry proved to be her "most fateful" letter.

Weight had no immediate plans, except that he wanted to write. Before the war he had been a Linotype operator in Eagle Rock, but he did not want to return to the printing trade. He had written fiction and non-fiction in his spare time which had been readily accepted for publication. Randall asked him to write for *Desert* and the Weight by-line began to appear regularly in 1946. His name appeared on the masthead of the magazine as associate editor (with Lucile) in the January, 1947, issue. Two months later Harold and Lucile were married. Harold continued to write regularly; eight of his gem collecting stories appeared in *Desert* during 1947. The newlyweds spent as much time as they could on field trips together, and they became ideal collaborators. Their specialty was the lore of lost mines and the stories of abandoned mining camps, although both had a profound knowledge of desert botany, minerals, history, and geography.

Harold preferred the freedom of free-lance writing to the tedium and detail of the editorial desk, and he resigned at the end of 1948, six months after the move to Palm Desert. After making their bases in San Diego and Pasadena while traveling and writing, they moved to Twentynine Palms. There Harold continued writing for *Westways, Desert, Pacific Discovery,* and other magazines, and later Lucile's by-line appeared in *Desert* and elsewhere. In 1950 they started publishing *Calico Print,* a unique monthly, later bi-monthly, a little magazine of history, legend, lost mines, ghost towns, and travel in the desert west. When they suspended it at the end of 1953 they continued publication of single titles on the desert's past, based on their research, travel, and tape-recorded interviews.

Harold is the author of a number of lost mine books of the desert southwest; one is now in its fifth edition, others in third and fourth editions.

Randall's loss of two skilled and imaginative associate editors at a critical time was a severe blow. His letters during the early 1950s indicate his fruitless efforts to find comparable replacements, although he maintained a cheerful optimism as he built his staff and increased his own working hours. Lucile and her correspondent, young people who met and married in the turbulence of their common interest, made significant and constructive editorial contributions to *Desert* Magazine, sharpening talents and experience which were useful when they decided to "go on their own."

SALT OF THE EARTH

When I reported for work at the Calexico *Chronicle* in 1930, the first voice I heard came from a smiling little woman whose shoulders barely cleared the counter where she stood. I learned her name was Mrs. Bess Stacy, and she had come to the *Chronicle* as bookkeeper two years earlier. She was a salty little personality, and her pungent remarks suggested an orderly mind with a marked sense of sly humor. She valued the integrity of her work and she had a strong sense of loyalty to persons and institutions she trusted.

Soon after I left the magazine Bess came to El Centro to assume the role of business manager, a job she continued to handle competently at Palm Desert until her retirement in 1958 when Randall sold the property. She had served faithfully as employee and stock-owning associate for thirty years.

During the difficult years of the early 1950s Bess often worked nights and weekends in order to carry more than her share of the work load. Randall often remarked that he didn't know what he would do without her faithfulness, courage, and good business sense. She died at Palm Desert in 1967 at the age of 85, leaving with her many friends a memory that she was indeed "the salt of the earth," a special member of the desert elite.

OL' BREEZY AT CERRO PRIETO

CHAPTER 6 begins with a paragraph about Ol' Breezy, the ancient vehicle I used for exploratory trips in 1930-32. In going through the files before me, I find a Letters page from *Desert* (December, 1948, page 4) which reproduces a picture of the jalopy and its pilot and a letter I wrote to Randall. I commented on the old car, recalled that the early magazine experience was probably the most exciting of my writing career, and concluded with these lines:

> *My scrapbook shows that the first of the weekly newspaper columns about my desert travels—which you attribute as the seed from which* Desert *grew—was published in the* Chronicle *October 16, 1930, just eighteen years to the day before the impressive opening of your new Palm Desert publishing plant. That first story was about a trip to the volcanic crater of Black Butte in Baja California.* MAC.

The Black Butte referred to is the Cerro Prieto described by Science Editor John Lear of *Saturday Review* (December 5, 1970) as one of the most promising geothermal areas of the western hemisphere. I am freshly reminded of my visit of forty-two years ago by a long article in the Winter 1971-72 issue of *Cry California* by Stanley Scott and Samuel E. Wood: "California's Bright Geothermal Future." It begins with this sentence: "California is virtually ignoring a major geothermal discovery, a vast supply of heat and water whose early and carefully controlled development would help alleviate a host of the state's critical environmental and economic problems."

The article describes world-wide tapping of great underground steam power sources, including Pacific Gas and Electric's Sonoma County system (presently 190 megawatts of electrical power) and Cerro Prieto, which the Mexican government has currently developed to a capacity of 75 megawatts. (One megawatt is one million watts, enough to light up a medium-sized town).

My first travelog required that I navigate rutted roads and ditch banks and do some foot-slogging through muddy fields in order to reach the lake of "solfateras" about twenty miles south of Mexicali. A paved highway now reaches the site. I saw no signs of human life or habitation. I tried to describe with some imagination the violent volcanism which perhaps millions of years ago built a great volcano (now inactive) and which still shows signs of subterranean life in the bubbling mudpots.

Another place I visited frequently when a resident of Calipatria was the "Mullet Island Mud Pots" at the southern tip of Salton Sea, an extension of the deep ridge structure that created Cerro Prieto. Scientists who have studied the area estimate that the Salton Trough (extending some miles from Mullet Island) contains perhaps ten billion acre feet of water at 400 to 600 degrees F., enough power, if harnessed, to stagger man's imagination.

I could not have imagined when I climbed the obsidian slopes of Black Butte that there was hidden power under foot that would eventually change the lives of millions of men in this part of the world. And I am not sure that any contemporary man can visualize the Coachella Valley of the future if and when man harnesses the electrical power and fresh water sources that lie under the crust of Imperial Valley.

This discovery and its potential would have delighted Randall because of the improved living conditions it portends for desert dwellers. But it would have saddened him, too, for

the implied population growth and paving over of the wastelands he loved.

LONG OVERDUE CORRECTIONS

SOMEBODY handed me a clipping out of Palm Desert *Post,*
a portion of a column written by a former sports figure. The
piece, printed in April, 1967, contained these two sentences:
"It is nice that Cliff Henderson was finally honored as
Palm Desert's "mayor" because it was Cliff and his late brother
Phil *and no one else* who started Palm Desert. My memory's
pretty good on some things, and while brother Randolph
Henderson has been around the desert since circa 1937, he
was moving to Arizona with his magazine until Cliff gave
him acreage to keep the magazine here and build a home for
it."
The writer of this fiction had a fallible memory. He didn't
remember how to spell the brother's name, nor did he "remember" that "Randolph" was well established as a desert resident
in 1911, twenty-six years before the date he dug up. His use
of the italic *and no one else* was planted with deliberate
malice, intended to discredit rather than enlighten.
Randall never claimed the sophistic title of "Father of
Palm Desert," nor did he presume to have created a community. He left a record of letters and legal documents which
verify completely his actions on site acquisition which ante-
ceded community development. Let the record stand; let
others take the credit for "Fatherhood," and whatever virtue
may be involved.
Another canard which deserves correction is that Randall
threatened to take *Desert* to another location unless he got the
twenty-acre grant specified in his deal with Cliff. It is true that
he had briefly explored alternate possibilities, but he had no
fixed plan to go to Arizona. He invited me to search with him

for land "somewhere near the palm canyons," and I am sure his thinking never wavered far from the Deep Canyon cove. He found Phoenix, Tucson, and Las Vegas too urban and nearby areas were overpriced or inappropriate for his purposes. His desert-worn boots turned instinctively toward the Deep Canyon cove overlooked by the Santa Rosas where seven years before we made our final decision to go ahead with the gamble of starting a regional magazine.

The Palm Desert Corporation, subdividers of the site, deeded a small parcel of land required by the publishing firm (and this initial largess no doubt provided a comfortable profit). Randall's interest was to have a trading center and a post office convenient to his publishing headquarters, but he was not necessarily dependent upon these factors. There's no denying that Cliff and Phil built a city (with a good deal of help from hundreds of investors). But how and why they came to the desert is fairly described in Chapter 5, without referral to pride in fatherhood.

A PLODDER WITH IMAGINATION

WHEN RANDALL went to his desk the morning after *Desert* Magazine settled in its new Palm Desert building, he found there a scroll of appreciation from his associates. It was addressed to "A Plodder with Imagination."

Desert's editor was indeed a plodder, but he was much more. Even after a time when most men are taking it easy he was spending long hours on the job. Although he did not easily delegate responsibility to others until the later years of his tenure, he appreciated industry in his associates. Even his approach to mountain climbing and river boating was marked by dogged determination and thoroughness; he liked to have arrangements for equipment preparation and time schedules well understood before starting a trip.

When he was disturbed or angry about something, his voice did not rise, nor did I ever hear him use profanity. His face would flush and his lips would draw thin and straight above a hard-set jaw. He often appeared to be humorless; witty speech or pleasantries did not come easily to him. He liked well-told tales, but he didn't want them off color. He liked the light touch in writing prose, but not for humor's sake.

Never fluent in speech, he avoided speaking engagements if he could. But when he sat at a campfire with friends or appeared before a group of young people at an informal outdoor setting, he could talk effectively, with conviction and empathy.

If he professed to eloquence at all, it showed briefly on his printed pages; many passages were perceptive and imaginative. He trained himself to be a good reporter and that is how he saw himself: matter-of-fact, no funny business, no disturbing obfuscation. His professional doctrine was "Let's get on with the story. Let's tell it so that readers will feel and appreciate, as well as know and understand."

A MAN MUST KNOW HIS TIME

IN THE SPRING of 1954 I drove the length of California in order to join Randall and two other men for an exploration trip into the mountains of Baja California. Our Mexican drivers dropped us off in a pine and juniper forest of the Sierra Juarez, a plateau about twenty miles south of Rumarosa, a tiny settlement on the Mexicali-Tijuana road. I've forgotten the name of the area we were to explore, but I think it was Cañon de los Tanques, a rugged gorge cutting the eastern slope of the sierra. Our rendezvous with the cars was set for two days later on the floor of Laguna Salada.

The 4000-foot descent was much rougher than we had anticipated. We worked downward between the walls of the canyon, skirting huge rocks and deep pools. Sheer dry water-falls forced us to retreat and detour many times. By midafter-noon of the second day our companions were far ahead. Randall and I were together when we reached a waterfall having a smooth granite face we estimated to be 120 feet to the base. We had only sixty feet of rope. We rested, talking without enthusiasm about the necessity of climbing out of the canyon in search of a climbable tributary. I saw Randall's shoulders sag, his head bowed in an attitude of prayer. As we sat there I suddenly realized this man was 66 years of age, and he had planned a physically exhausting trip with men in their 40s. After a few minutes, he turned and spoke to me.

"Mac," he said, "there must come a time in every man's life when he must know that he has reached the end of his trail; he must find easier and safer routes to get where he must go. I think in this hour I've come near the end of my trail. I'll leave my pack here. I don't want it to hold us back."

There was weariness in his voice, but no despair and no melodrama. After a few minutes I heard a matter-of-fact "Okay, Mac, I'm ready to move now." I had insisted on taking his camera and a few personal things, but he left his bedroll and grubsack on the mountain. We moved out steadily in the growing darkness, the moonlight aiding us over the last few miles down the sandy floor of the wide bajada. It was a wel-come sight to see the campfire of our friends at the edge of the ancient lakebed.

That moment of revelation on the mountain told me much about my friend. He had long called himself a heretic, but he had a profound belief in the Creator of the natural world. He also had confidence in his own strength to master anything he set out to do. He had always competed against himself. From his wrestling championships in college, through the grim challenges of his early newspaper experiences in desert towns, to difficult mountain climbing treks, he had never doubted his capacity to win the test. When his strength ebbed he knew what he could do with what remained. He never climbed a mountain again. But he continued to follow trails of his choosing, resulting in publication of two revealing books on his desert experiences, released in 1962 and 1968.

BEAUTY AS WELL AS BREAD

JACK PEPPER interviewed Randall for an article which appeared in the March, 1964, issue of *Desert*— the month Pepper became publisher of the magazine. Randall commented that the people who made him the most intolerant were those who desecrated the desert he so loved, and he quoted a favorite line written by Naturalist John Muir:

Everybody needs beauty as well as bread, places to play in and pray in, where Nature may heal and cheer and give strength to body and soul alike.

Randall then went on to expand his thought on this subject:

"That was true when John Muir lived. It is a truth of even greater significance today, for these are confusing times. While humans push and crowd and burn themselves out in a crazy stampede for more profits and higher wages and the satisfaction of personal vanities, Nature goes along in her own serene way, undisturbed by the petty bickerings of the passing parade of homo sapiens."

This and additional quotations from Randall's writings appeared in a long obituary, *In Memory of "Mr. Desert,"* which Pepper wrote for the September, 1970, issue of *Desert*.

DEATH VALLEY FORTYNINER

From its inception, Randall had been an active participant in the programs of Death Valley '49ers, Inc. Mary DeDecker of Independence, California, long-time booster

of the organization, wrote me the following letter, apolo-
gizing for delay because "it is not easy to dig up anything
showy; Randall was not that kind of man."

"THE PURPOSE of the organization was to protect and interpret the Death Valley area, to further public understanding
of that part of the desert country that meant so much to
Randall. He could truly put his heart into supporting these
objectives.

"The organization had been formed for the purpose of
producing an appropriate centennial pageant in Death Valley
to illustrate the poignant drama which had taken place there
a hundred years ago. The overwhelming public response to
this event convinced the '49er directors that it should be kept
alive. Randall was one of the directors, and he had a part in
setting the standards in those formative years. The programs
were to be true to the arid west—no carnival types of amuse-
ments—emphasis to be on the history, cultures, and natural
features of the region. As a frequent chairman of the author's
breakfast, he brought in writers who helped interpret the
desert story. When the time came that he could not continue
in such an active role, Randall was named an honorary director in 1964. Perhaps his greatest contribution he made that
same year when he detected and thwarted a movement within
the organization which he believed to be a flagrant reversal of
principle. His courage and determination in taking a minority
stand eventually won a majority vote.

"Randall's integrity was a shining light whenever principles were at stake. Quiet courage was a part of his being.
His subtle contributions to the well-being of the Death Valley
'49ers would be difficult to measure."

THERE ARE TWO DESERTS

In the summer of 1936 Randall wrote an editorial of nine paragraphs which he printed in a dummy and prospectus of a proposed Desert Magazine. *It was to be another thirteen months before the original printing appeared again in the first issue of* Desert, *bearing both of our names as publishers. I approved it, but did not join in the writing. The original printing was under an EDITORIAL heading, and the subtitle was "The Plan and Mission of the Desert Magazine." That 800-word piece remained the basic editorial policy of the magazine during the twenty-one years of Randall's editorship, although only the first three paragraphs were used countless times in newspaper and magazine articles about Randall's career.*

THERE ARE TWO DESERTS. One is a grim desolate wasteland. It is the home of venomous reptiles and stinging insects, of vicious thorn-covered plants and trees, and of unbearable heat. This is the desert seen by the stranger speeding along the highway, impatient to be out of "this damnable country." It is the desert visualized by those children of luxury to whom any environment is unbearable which does not provide all of the comforts and services of a pampering civilization. It is the concept fostered by fiction writers who dramatize the tragedies of the desert country for the profit it will bring them.

But the stranger and the uninitiated see only the mask. The other desert— the real desert is not for the eyes of the superficial observer, nor the fearful soul or the cynic. It is a land whose character is hidden except to those who come with friendliness and understanding. To these the desert offers rare gifts: health-giving sunshine, a night sky that is studded with diamonds, a breeze that bears no poison, a landscape of pastel colors such as no artist can duplicate, thorn-covered plants which during countless ages have clung tenaciously to life through heat and drought and wind and the depredations of thirsty animals, and yet each season send forth blossoms of exquisite coloring as a symbol of courage that has triumphed over terrifying obstacles.

To those who come to the desert with friendliness, it gives friendship. To those who come with courage, it gives strength of character. Those seeking relaxation find release from the world of man-made troubles. For those seeking beauty, the desert offers nature's rarest artistry. This is the desert men and women learn to love.

REFERENCES

(Bibliography of sources used in writing Chapters 2, 3, and 4)

Barrows, David Prescott. *The Ethno-botany of the Cahuilla Indians of Southern California.* Univ. of Chicago Press 1900, 87 pp. Republished 1967 by Malki Museum, Inc., Banning, Calif.

Bell, Horace. *Reminiscences of a Ranger.* Yarnell, Caystile & Mather, Printers, Los Angeles, 1881, 457 pp.

Chase, J. Smeaton. *California Desert Trails.* Houghton Mifflin Co., New York, 1919, 387 pp.

Cleland, Robert Glass. *From Wilderness to Empire.* Alfred A. Knopf, New York, 1944, 388 pp.

Cory, H.T. *The Imperial Valley and the Salton Sink.* Introductory monograph by W.P. Blake. John J. Newbegin, San Francisco, 1915, 377 pp.

Imperial Irrigation District. *Historic Salton Sea and Imperial Irrigation District.* 1960, 32 pp.

James, Harry C. *The Cahuilla Indians.* Foreword by M.R. Harrington. Westernlore Press, Los Angeles, 1960, 185 pp. Republished 1969 by Malki Museum Press, Banning, Calif.

James, George Wharton. *Wonders of the Colorado Desert.* T.F. Unwin, London, 1906, 547 pp.

Nordland, Ole J. *Coachella Valley's Golden Years.* Coachella Valley County Water District, 1968, 88 pp.

Kroeber, A.L. *Ethnography of the Cahuilla Indians.* University of California Press, 1908.

Patencio, Francisco. (As told to Margaret Boynton) *Stories and Legends of the Palm Springs Indians.* Palm Springs Desert Museum, 1943, 88 pp.

Ryan, R. Mark. *Mammals of Deep Canyon, Colorado Desert, California.* Palm Springs Desert Museum, 1968, 138 pp.

Van Dyke, John C. *The Desert.* Charles Scribner's Sons, New York. 1912, 233 pp.